The Pocket Therapist, II.

The Pocket Therapist, II.

David A. Brown, Ph.D.

iUniverse, Inc.
New York Lincoln Shanghai

The Pocket Therapist, II.

All Rights Reserved © 2003 by David A. Brown, Ph.D.

No part of this book may be reproduced or transmitted in any form or by any means, graphic, electronic, or mechanical, including photocopying, recording, taping, or by any information storage retrieval system, without the written permission of the publisher.

iUniverse, Inc.

For information address:
iUniverse, Inc.
2021 Pine Lake Road, Suite 100
Lincoln, NE 68512
www.iuniverse.com

ISBN: 0-595-30542-3

Printed in the United States of America

Contents

Chad Cannot Be Rotten 1
    Chad learns he can become a rotten little boy; or can he?

Puppets 6
    Are we emotional Puppets? Who pulls our strings?

Stinky 13
    He was so afraid of the devil that he would not play in the garden.

Fake It…Till You Make It! 18
    Is it really possible to change habits? How can red poker chips help?

Candy 28
    Her mother could upset her whenever she wanted, and keep her that way!

The Death Call 39
    "Now, Dr. Brown, how do you feel having heard your wife died?

This Isn't Really Happening To Me! 42
    "I found my daughter in the backseat with three young men!"

The Night After Thanksgiving 49
    They were controlling each other. I wanted to rescue the helpless female!

Mister Ghost 52
    It was a little scary, but Austin knew what he had to do.

"Mom" Nelson 57
    I really didn't want to be one of the two-thirds!

Kim 61
    …a ten-year-old, Arizona, female, tarantula spider?

"If You Do, What You've Always Done, You'll Get What You Always Got" 65
    Butchers have a tendency to cheat women!

Tootsie Pop Therapy 67
    The awesome power of a Tootsie Pop!

Yes I Can! 71
    "I am an illegitimate person with no right to happiness!"

Feelings 75
    They are the joy we search for and the suffering we experience.

To Achieve My Dreams, Practice These ABC's 80
    You are unique, worthwhile, loveable, special, powerful and trainable.

About The Author 81

Acknowledgements

I want to express my gratitude to the woman and man who gave me a chance to experience life, Dorothy and Lawrence Brown. They did everything possible to give me a loving and healthy beginning. My mentors were many and varied. Some were especially remarkable. When I think of the teachings in this book, I fondly remember Mrs. Margaret "Mom" Nelson, my English professor, who told me I had a gift for writing. I also remember my philosophy professor, Dr. George Axtelle. His words to me were profound and his friendship powerful. Dr. Viktor Frankl brought special meaning to my life in his classes in San Diego. "If I don't do it, who will do it? If I don't do it now, when will it be done? And, if I do it only for myself, what am I?" Dr. Bill Wilkins taught me about the healing forces involved in the counseling relationship. Dr. Maxie Maultsby, Jr. shared Rational Behavior Therapy and the locus of human emotional control with me. Dr. Albert Ellis has been an inspiration, mentor and friend, along with Dr. Maultsby since 1973. Their teachings changed me forever. My sons, David and Chad, are two more of the great men I know and love. They are two of the greatest gifts I've received in my life. Their lives remind me everyday of the joy, and responsibility, of parenthood. My wife, Marcia, is my best friend and partner. I am thankful everyday for her love and friendship. Thoughts of her remind me daily that there is nothing more important in the world than love.

I would be remiss not to thank the thousands of patients and students that have helped shape my life. Each and every one seems to insist that I look deeper inside myself for truth and wisdom. And often, *they* are indeed the educator. Thank you!

Chad Cannot Be Rotten

Not long ago, Chad and his brother, and his Mom and Dad, moved to a new house. The new house was in a new town, a long, long, way from their old house.

Chad liked his old house, and his old school, and friends. He had no idea at all what the new house would be like. He'd rather not move but the whole family was moving, and he didn't want to stay at the old house by himself.

His Dad was happy going to a new job, his Mother was happy going to a new house, and his brother was happy because he would have his own bedroom.

Chad decided to be happy too.

When he saw the new house he liked it. Chad liked the big yard, and the cornfield across the road. He liked the rickety wooden bridge across the creek, just down the road from his new home. He liked the whole world.

When Chad's Mom enrolled him at Hilltop School he went gladly, and he liked it. He met some new kids, and he thought they were "super".

The world was just the way it should be. When he went to sleep at night he just scrunched right down into the pillow. He liked to fall asleep fast and dream about building a dam across the creek.

In the morning, he liked to think about all the good stuff he would do during the day.

During the second week of school, his teacher explained a kind of game they were going to play. There was a big red apple hung on the bulletin board for each pupil in the class. If a pupil misbehaved, the teacher would put a little brown worm on the apple. If the apple accumulated five worms it would be called a rotten apple and fall to the ground. The rotten apple student would get a spanking in front of the class.

None of this made too much of an impression on Chad. Nobody was going to misbehave! And nobody would get spanked in school! It was just one of those things that grown-ups talk about.

One day while Miss Miller was out of the classroom one of the boys stood up and whispered real loud, "Miss Miller is a diller". Chad didn't think that made any sense, but everyone laughed when they heard it. So, he stood up and said,

"Miss Miller is a diller". The unfortunate thing was that Miss Miller walked into the classroom just as he said it!

She was upset. She definitely believed that little boys should not poke fun at their teachers. Chad could tell by looking at her face that she was displeased. He wished he hadn't stood up and said, "Miss Miller is a diller".

"Chad", said Miss Miller, "I can tell that you want a rotten apple. You certainly earned a worm by being bad today!" With that she took a brown worm out of her desk and pasted it on the apple with Chad's name on it.

Some of the children laughed when they saw this. Chad laughed too, to show that he wasn't worried—but he was worried. He didn't know how he had gotten into such a predicament.

He liked Miss Miller. He liked her from the very first time he saw her. Now she had put a worm on his apple and he thought that they weren't friends any more. He wished he could go home. He wished he didn't have to stay in school. He didn't like having a rotten apple.

At recess he didn't feel like playing catch with his friends. He sat and watched. They seemed to be having a good time without him. He thought how lucky those kids were, not having worms on their apples as he did.

From that day on, Chad was very, very, careful not to do anything that Miss Miller might get upset about. He certainly did not want another worm on his apple. School wasn't fun anymore. It was mostly trying to stay out of trouble.

While Chad worried about staying out of trouble, and worried about getting another worm, other children were not so lucky. John Slocum got in trouble every day. By the middle of the second week he had five worms on his apple. The teacher let the rotten apple fall off the bulletin board and land on the floor. Then John Slocum had to come to the front of the room and Miss Miller gave him a spanking.

Chad was horrified.

John Slocum shed a few tears.

Chad dreamed about a rotten apple that night. He tried to pin it back on the bulletin board but it kept falling off.

The next morning Chad did not want to go to school. He didn't want to even look at his apple with the worm on it. When his mother asked him why he didn't want to go to school he said it was because he felt rotten.

Chad's mother decided that he wasn't sick and that he should go to school.

The children were surprised to find that all of the apples had been taken down from the bulletin board! One of the little girls whose apple didn't have any worms on it asked Miss Miller where the apples were. Miss Miller replied, "I don't know what I have to do to get you children to behave, but the apples did not work, so I will have to think of something else."

Chad was delighted.

John Slocum hollered, "HOORAY!" real loud, and Miss Miller looked very stern.

It wasn't long before Miss Miller did think of something else. The fact that Thanksgiving was approaching gave her the idea. She pasted pretty pumpkin faces all around the room, one for each pupil. Chad's name was on one of the pumpkins. Chad smiled a big smile. His pumpkin smiled a big smile back. Chad felt comfortable. Every-time he looked at his pumpkin it was looking right back at him.

At recess, John Slocum was over by the book cabinet and Miss Miller told him to take his seat. He didn't hear her. Miss Miller told him a second time to take his seat. He heard her that time and said, "Okay, Miss Miller," but stayed at the book cabinet to finish whatever it was he was doing.

Miss Miller went over to John's pumpkin and plucked off one of its eyebrows. "You can just take home a horrible looking pumpkin at Thanksgiving because you are a horrible boy," said Miss Miller. "How can I get this class to behave if no one will listen!" she complained.

Poor John Slocum watched his pumpkin disappear during the next two weeks. Once he pushed a girl, not purposely of course, and he had trouble with talking when Miss Miller wanted to talk. All the while Poor Chad thought continuously about how he wanted to escape having his pumpkin destroyed.

Now, he didn't want to go to school, and was usually sick when it was time to go. He especially liked Saturdays, Sundays, and days when there were teacher's meetings. He was now uncomfortable in school with his pumpkin looking down at him.

Miss Miller told Chad that she wished he would talk a little louder when she spoke to him. He always answered her very, very, quietly, and most of the time he sort of turned his head sideways so he could have his pumpkin in sight. So Miss Miller had trouble hearing him when he answered in class. But, he didn't want his pumpkin to look rotten, with maybe a missing nose or eyebrow. He even sat down quietly, not banging his seat like some other kids.

Chad never worried too much about what Miss Miller was teaching. He figured that was far less important than protecting his pumpkin which, thank goodness, was still whole.

Miss Miller decided that Chad was just a daydreamer, and his report card was marked to show that he did not pay attention.

Chad's Mom and Dad talked to him about his report card, and his reluctance to go to school and his lack of interest in school activities. Then they talked to some of the other parents. The pupils did not want to be rotten in school and bring home rotten pumpkins to their parents! Getting a rotten pumpkin and having the other kids call you rotten was no fun at all!

The children in Miss Miller's class were very much surprised to come to school one day and find that all the pumpkins had been taken down and were nowhere to be found. They asked Miss Miller about the missing pumpkins. She said that she had taken them down and that the pupils were not to concern themselves with <u>why</u> they were down. Chad didn't know what was wrong, but he knew <u>something</u> was wrong. He wished that he lived in Willie Wonka's Chocolate Factory.

When the first snow fell, Miss Miller gave the children some construction paper and they each made a snowman to hang on the classroom wall. When Chad made the mouth on his snowman he made it straight across, and the snowman looked rather sad that way. Chad wished he had made the mouth curved up so that the snowman would look smiley.

Even after the snowmen were hung, Chad wished he had made the mouth smiley. He asked Miss Miller if he could make the snowman's head over again. Miss Miller said he shouldn't bother because by the time Christmas came most of the snowmen wouldn't have hats, or heads, or arms, because of the rotten children and the rotten way they behaved in class.

I'm going to take home a rotten snowman home at Christmas time, thought Chad. He looked at the snowman, and it looked sadder than when he made it. Instead of the mouth being straight across it seemed to droop a little bit at the corners!

On Saturday morning, Chad's father asked him why he was moping around instead of going out to play with his best friend. "I feel rotten," Chad said, because by Christmas time my snowman will be rotten and I won't want to bring it home."

"Chad," said his father, "I love you, and your happiness is important to me. I want you to come outside by the basketball hoop for a minute." Chad went out with his father. His father tossed the basketball to Chad and said, "Let's see you make ten baskets in a row." Chad laughed and said, "I can't do that, you know. I'm not a champ basketball player." He tossed the ball, and missed, and tried again, and missed, and then the third time he made a basket. His father said, "Now you see son, you missed the basket a couple of times, but that does not mean you are a rotten person."

"I would like for you to behave as intelligently as you can, be as wise as you know how, and just do your best at school and at play. There is no sense trying to figure out who is the rottenest kid in your class."

"You can easily figure out who plays ball the best, or who spells the best, or who has the biggest feet. There is nothing wrong with that."

"But picking the rottenest kid is **NOT** in your best interest. There is **NO SUCH THING** as a rotten person."

"There may be rotten apples, but **NOT** rotten human beings! Instead of worrying, it would be so much better if you would just quit measuring who is rottenest and simply go to school and know that you are Chad. Just be Chad!"

"If you have a spelling bee and don't do well in it, you can tell yourself that you didn't spell well. You won't have to worry about being a rotten person, you can just choose to study spelling a little bit more."

"If people tell you that you are rotten, you will know better than to believe them because you and I know that **YOU CANNOT BE ROTTEN**, no matter what. The same thing applies if they tell you that you are bad or horrible. It is just not true!"

"You will always be Chad, no matter how you behave!"

Chad **CANNOT** Be Rotten! And, neither can you!

Food For Thought

- Have <u>you</u> ever felt rotten, or thought <u>you</u> were risking becoming rotten because of something you did? What were the circumstances?

- Was it <u>you</u> who was being critical of <u>your</u> behavior, or was it someone else? What was being said about you?

- How would <u>you</u> handle the situation today? How would your thinking change today? Please be specific with your response.

Puppets

Article Saves Life: This story has an interesting history. After a radio interview, Dr. Dave left this story on the coffee table in the lobby as he was leaving the station. The station manager had planned to commit suicide that very evening. For reasons he could not explain, he noticed the paper as he left the building that evening and put it in his pocket. As he began to take his overdoes of medication and drink the bourbon he bought on his way home that night, he started to read his copy of Puppets. He stopped attempting to die and called me on Monday morning to report that he was "alive and wanted to talk." He said the paper gave him the idea that "he had choices he never before believed."

Habits are those forces within us that direct us to behave the same way in the same situation. We learn to drink coffee in the morning before we do anything else. We learn that coffee is just not complete without a cylinder of paper stuffed with tobacco. We learn our habits so very well that soon we awake in the morning and are so well programmed that we find we are at work before we even realize that we are awake. We take a shower, brush our teeth, comb our hair, put on all those pastes and liquids, and never really stop to think about what we _really_ want to do each step of the way. We simply practice till we have the procedure down so pat that we do not have to think about it any longer.

We learn to smoke and soon realize that every time we answer the phone we also automatically reach into our shirt pocket and search for a cigarette, without really wanting or deciding to have a cigarette. Answering the phone means to also have a cigarette. In fact, we find that on days when we have to answer the phone a great deal, we also smoke a great deal. That strange "force within us" has again taken over and we are once again puppets.

I am reminded of an old friend who used to bite his fingernails. He bit them with such vigor that his nails would no longer be bitable, so he would bite his skin. In fact, he bit his skin with such vigor that his fingers would bleed. I questioned him as to why he would continue to do that. I asked if it felt good? He said, "Of course not! It hurts, but it is a habit and I cannot stop!" It was clear to my friend, that this "strange inner force" had taken over his mouth and his teeth and he was unable to stop placing his fingers in his mouth...he was forced to bite and bite. Imagine this situation. My friend was unable to control his mouth, teeth and the muscles of his arms. His fingers were automatically placed in his mouth and he <u>had</u> to bite himself. Now that you have read these words for the second time I hope you understand his ridiculous attitude.

My friend was, in fact, <u>in control</u> of his hands. He did not have to bite himself. He <u>learned</u> to do this to himself at certain times, like when he was faced with a problem for which he did not have a quick solution. He practiced chewing on his fingers whenever he was nervous and the habit took over. When he was nervous, or thought he had a problem, he bit his nails. Soon he was "biting without thinking."

My friend believes that he has <u>always</u> bitten his nails, that he "is a nervous person", and he will always be a person who bites his nails. He is out of control! The habit has taken over! He got to the point of embarrassing himself with his nail-biting, so he hides his face and hands behind a book in order to let his habit continue without other people seeing what he is doing.

That is just the beginning of the list of habits that are out of control for human beings. How about these? "I cannot stop smoking, drinking alcohol, worrying about my children, arguing with my wife, eating candy, fighting with my roommate, driving too fast, thinking that others dislike me, crying when I see an animal hurt, getting angry when someone calls me a name, talking in class, getting into trouble with my teacher, believing that San Francisco will fall into the sea, thinking that I would be a better person if I had more self-confidence, wishing that I were rich, or wishing my spouse would behave as I want." We all have our own personal list of habits that "control us" and that we "cannot break."

The result of these attitudes is that we are "creatures of habit" and therefore "controlled by our habits." We are **<u>PUPPETS</u>** and should stop fighting these inner forces because they are always going to be within us and we might as well learn to live with them.

We could <u>choose</u> to not be satisfied being **<u>PUPPETS</u>** and learn to change our behavior. We can learn to behave, as we really would like to behave. We can make our habits work <u>for</u> us rather than against us.

I asked my friend whether he wanted to continue to be a finger-biting-puppet or whether he wanted to admit that he really did control what he put into his mouth...did he want to learn to stop biting himself? At this point, he chose not to get angry with me for referring to him as a puppet, and asked a question of me. He said, "You just used the word 'learned.' You said that I <u>learned</u> to bite my nails? So are you implying that I can <u>learn</u> not to bite myself?" I said that he was either <u>born</u> biting his nails <u>or</u> he learned this habit <u>after</u> birth. He could understand that when he was in the nursery as an infant, he probably did not bite his nails. Indeed, he remembered how he had started to bite his nails in college when the work got too intense. He could remember a time when he did not have the habit.

His new insight was that he <u>learned</u> to do something (bite his nails), and, therefore, he could <u>learn</u> not to do the very same thing. And so it is that we can change habits because (1) we once did not have the habit, and (2) we remember learning the behavior. We can rid ourselves of habits that we do not like. We can learn to have habits that are more in our best interest.

This means that there is <u>no</u> strange, uncontrollable force active within us to make us do things that we do not want to do. We learn to act the way we do and we can, at any time, learn to behave differently.

My friend soon understood that he did <u>not</u> have to put his fingers in his mouth, and he did <u>not</u> have to bite himself. He could learn to keep his fingers out of his mouth and use his energy to do something he would enjoy. So it is with physical habits. We can train ourselves, through practice, to bite our nails, or not.

Are you thinking that this news is not really new to you? Are you thinking that it is very clear to you that <u>you</u> control where you put your hands, where you sit, when you stand, where you walk, and so on? If you were, I would say that most people probably agree with you. We learn physical habits and we can un-learn physical habits.

There are, however, two other categories of human behavior. The second is "cognitive" or "thinking" behavior. What about the thinking habits that we have...can we change our attitudes and beliefs? What about when you hear that people with a certain skin color are dangerous? We hear this from enough people and we may soon form the thinking habit, called an attitude or belief, that people with that particular skin color really are dangerous. Therefore the next time we see a person with that skin color we get frightened. We say, "that person frightened us!" but it was really our attitude that caused the fright.

We may think that mushrooms are bad to eat and we stay away from them and don't eat any. We think that people who like to read are not as worthy as people who play football and we see little value in the "bookworm." We think that college is too hard so we quit and never really give ourselves an opportunity to be successful. We think that teachers are people who are out to get us and we start to fight with them from the very beginning. We think that people with lots of money are better people than people with little money. We think, and we think, and we form attitudes that help us, and some that work against us. I can remember thinking that I could not climb a mountain and so I never tried. One day I challenged that self-defeating belief and asked, "I think I can't and so I don't! But, I wonder if I could climb a mountain if I thought I could?" I began to practice the thought that I most likely <u>could</u> climb a mountain if I had a mountain, the proper equipment, and the information as to how to climb. I went to North Carolina and asked the Outward Bound School to let me use their Table Rock. Indeed, I climbed the mountain and did it well!

I had lots of challenging thoughts after that. I started to challenge lots of attitudes I had about myself. I found many of them were highly inaccurate. I could do far more than I believed possible at the time. At least I could make the effort to find out.

Thus far we have discussed two of the three categories of human behavior. I know that I have both physical and cognitive habits, learned patterns of behavior that can be helpful or harmful. I know that I have learned to think and behave in ways that are in my best interest and that are self-defeating. And, I know that I have <u>choices</u> about how I think and physically behave. I can change my thoughts and my physical behavior. I am in charge of my thinking and my physical behavior!

The third classification of human behavior is emotive, or emotional behavior. My brain also exercises ultimate control over my emotional behavior. This is where my friend started to disagree with me once again. He said that he found it impossible to believe that if someone called him a jackass he would not get angry. "In fact," he said, "I would go so far as to say that if someone calls me a jackass I <u>have</u> to get angry!" Let's look at this idea. He said that he has to get angry if someone says something to him that he does not like. Let's go back to the nursery for a moment. Let's imagine that we walk into a hospital nursery where newborn babies are waiting to be taken home. We walk into the nursery and say, "All you kids in here are a bunch of jackasses!" If the word "jackass" can make a human being angry then all the babies would be angry with us for calling them such a name. Of course this will not be the case. Do you know why? The babies will not be angry because they haven't <u>learned</u> to upset <u>themselves</u> having heard such a name. That's correct! I said <u>they have not yet learned to upset themselves</u> about the words that other people say to them. It's not the words that have magical power over another human being, but it's what we have <u>learned to think about</u> what other people say that causes our upset.

When I am sad, it is because I have learned a habit of upsetting myself when certain things happen around me. I learned to upset myself when someone I think is pretty tells me that she does not want to date me. I learned to upset myself when I don't get what I want. If I ask for a date and get the date, then I say "she made me happy." But I am the one that was in charge of my happiness because I could have chosen to be happy no matter what response I received. I could have said that I would like or prefer to have a date with this woman, but it would not be awful or terrible if she says no. If I tell myself that she <u>must</u> say "yes" if I ask her or I will be rejected and less of a man, then I will cause myself needless pain and suffering. I cause my pain and suffering depending on my own expectations and what I tell myself must happen.

Suppose that someone you define as "ugly" tells you she loves you. You will most likely not be happy with that pronouncement. If <u>words of love</u> make people happy, then you would be happy and not have a choice. You indeed have a choice in this case. You can be thrilled or frightened silly depending upon what you are saying to yourself about this person who says she loves you.

I remember the time a girlfriend told me that I made her happy when I gave her a box of candy. She actually made <u>herself</u> happy when I gave her the candy because <u>she</u> liked candy <u>and</u> she had a habit of thinking nice thoughts when someone gave her candy. Once she was on a secret diet to lose a few pounds to impress me with the way she looked. I went to see her with another box of candy, because the first box made such a positive impression. This time she got angry with me for being "so uncaring when she was working so very hard to diet!" She blamed me for upsetting her? It was really <u>her thoughts</u>, and not the sugar in a cardboard box, that were upsetting her. She did not know that <u>she</u> is responsible for the way <u>she</u> feels emotionally. She thought that <u>I</u> was in charge of her emotional life. The problem with that kind of thinking is that she will suffer needlessly. It is possible to be on a diet, receive a box of candy and not be upset. One could choose to save the candy for a later date. One could choose to be honest and explain that they are on a diet and the candy is only a negative temptation at the present time. One could accept the candy, throw it away and act appreciative. There are many choices other than upsetting oneself about a box of candy. And so it is with our emotional lives, we have many, many choices about what to think, and therefore how to feel.

We learn our habits…physical, cognitive and emotional. We can change the responses that we presently make. Just as we do not have to bite our nails, we do not have to be sad, angry, miserable and depressed when we do not want to be. People with healthy brains have control over all three areas of their behavior. Even when we think we are "out of control," we are really in control of how we are physically behaving, thinking and feeling.

The exciting fact is that we are <u>not</u> puppets controlled by our emotional habits, even when we think we are. We have control and we have choices! We can learn to exercise more efficient and effective control whenever we choose.

Allow me to explore one more idea with you. Imagine thinking that you are a "stupid person." You think and think and rethink the words, "I am a stupid person." If you practice this thought, you will eventually believe it. You will behave more and more like a stupid person should behave. You will behave in ways that support your thinking. You will come to <u>believe</u> that you <u>are</u> a stupid person even though you are not. You will be the same person you always were, but with a different attitude (thinking habit). You will now be the **_PUPPET_** of your "stupid habit." Your new attitude that you are stupid will keep you from trying things you'd like to attempt. Do you see what you have done? You have given yourself a new habit based on lies and you are using the lies to keep yourself from being successful.

Remember the mountain I wanted to climb? I told myself that I would love to try it but I am just not a mountain-climbing person! I told myself that I was not a mountain-climbing person and that belief kept me away from mountains. It became an attitude and therefore I never attempted to accomplish my desire. One day I examined my attitude regarding the kind of person who could climb a mountain. I thought about mountain climbing people. They had two legs, two arms, the proper equipment, a mountain and some mountain-climbing instructions. I had two legs, two arms, I could buy the needed equipment and I could borrow a mountain. I could indeed be "that kind of mountain-climbing person" whenever I wanted to be! Now I am!!

Have you read the book entitled <u>The Little Engine That Could</u>? The little train engine found that it could do much more than it ever thought possible if it practiced the thought, "I think I can, I think I can, I think I can!" I am not suggesting that you and I can do "anything" we think we can or "everything" we think we can. However, there is something that I have learned for myself, and that is that <u>I am capable of doing far more than I ever thought possible</u>. My potential is greater than I think. I bet there are still things I believe to be impossible that I could do, and do well. After successfully climbing Table Rock I know that my potential is far greater than I ever thought possible. That is exciting for me. It can be exciting for you also.

I believe that I can change the way I feel. I do not have to feel badly when others expect or demand I do. You can also believe that you can change the way you feel and you do not have to feel badly when others expect or demand you do.

You can do more than you believe possible at the present time. Give yourself a chance. Give yourself a new attitude. Try this one. Say "I <u>can</u> do <u>more</u> than I believe possible at the moment. I am <u>willing</u> to give myself the opportunity. I have <u>lots</u> of <u>choices</u>. I am a <u>powerful</u> person. I <u>can</u> change the way I <u>think</u>. I can <u>change</u> the way I behave. I can <u>change</u> my attitudes about the world and me, anytime I choose. I am a <u>valuable</u> human being and I <u>deserve</u> to treat myself better. I will start <u>now</u>!

Food For Thought

- Describe a habit that you would choose to modify, or eliminate completely, that has you behaving like a puppet.

- Why have you believed you have little or no control over the behavior?

- After reading this story, what have you learned that might give you the ability to change your seemingly unchangeable habit? Please be specific.

Stinky

It was a cold, dark, winter's day in Indiana. The lobby of the mental health center was filled with patients waiting to be helped. They were people in need of many things. They lacked coping skills; they lacked meaning in their lives; they lacked understanding; and they hurt.

Among the adults sat a young lad of ten years. His aunt was a patient at the center and had come there on a weekly basis for the past three years. She had a need she believed was being met by her therapist, and she continued to come for treatment. She believed she was being helped, and she wanted the same compassionate treatment for her nephew. She saw much of herself in the young man and was afraid for him, She didn't want him to go through what she had experienced in her young life. She cared about him and his future and wanted to help end his hurt before it got worse. She had seen the adults in her life as people who did not understand, and she now wanted to present herself to her nephew as someone who understood. She understood better than most, and she brought the young man to her doctor for advice and help.

"Stinky," as the boy was called, was afraid. He had lost 28 pounds recently, pounds that he could not afford. The laughter of youth was gone from his face. He was so very serious. He was shaking, not only on the inside like so many adults, but also on the outside where it could be noticed and not easily ignored. His face gave evidence of anxiety. He was not enjoying the heritage of his age, but was dealing with problems with which he could not cope. He was suffering and his aunt knew it. She brought him to see her therapist against his mother's wishes. She remembered that as a child she had begged for help and no one had listened. She told of the endless hours and days when she was alone with her thoughts and had no sympathetic listeners to share them. She well remembered her hurt and she wanted help for her young friend, help that she had not been able to find until late in life.

She begged, "Please help Stinky. He needs someone to talk to and confide in, someone who will listen and not punish him for his fears. He feels very much alone. I have tried to help him, but I just hurt with him and I'm not able to help. I cannot find the words necessary to change his beliefs. He knows that I care about him and yet I am not able to help ease the pain. You must help Stinky and me! Please!"

What must be done? It was evident that this young man was in need of help. He reminded the mental health professional of a milk shake machine in the old Dairy Dell where he enjoyed milk shakes as a boy. There as no doubt that something was being stirred up. The little boy shook and he looked at the therapist and said, "I'm, scared. I can't sleep at night. I throw up my food and my mother is mad at me. When I'm afraid, my mother and grandmother send me to my bedroom and tell me to stay there till I'm better and then I may come out of my room. They don't understand that I'm scared."

The therapist invited the boy into his office and asked him what was wrong. Stinky said that he had been going to church for the past two months at his mother's request and that was the beginning of his problems. He said the preacher told the children that they must not sin. They were not to be bad, and they were not to make mistakes or the punishment would be something that they would never forget. Stinky told the therapist of an evil thing that lived beneath the ground. It watched for boys and girls who made mistakes and did bad things. It could, and would, reach up out of the earth and grab them and pull them down into the fiery depths of the earth, never to be seen again. It was a bad thing! It was called "the devil" and it lurked in the shadows waiting for young boys and girls to be bad, and took them home with him. Stinky had never seen this devil but he *believed* that it existed and he was afraid of it.

Stinky remembered no sermons about the "love of God" or "the understanding of adults," but he remembered clearly the presence of the devil. He was afraid to go to school and he was afraid to play with his friends. It was not very hard to be bad and therefore it would not be very hard to be pulled into the center of the earth by that bad thing that was constantly after him. He had to always be on his guard and that was not fun. He was very, very frightened!

Stinky had heard adults speak of this creature. He didn't want to be hurt, and he didn't want to spend the rest of eternity in the center of the earth with the creature either. He shook! He cried!

The therapist told him that there are adults who know of no other way to get little people to behave than by scaring them. He told Stinky that when he was a little boy, there was a "boogie man." The Boogie Man worked for the sanitation department and rode the garbage truck every week and collected the garbage in the city. He was the same person who took bad little girls and boys with him when he came around to collect the garbage. But there was something wrong with that story. The therapist knew plenty of little boys and girls who did things that were "wrong," and the Boogie Man never picked them up. They were still on the block. They stole candy from the corner grocery and lied to their parents and cheated on tests in school and the Boogie Man never came to get them. It was all a fairy tale. It was the way the adults tried to get kids to do what THEY wanted. There was no Boogie Man. There *were* parents who could punish their children. There were teachers who could punish them for misbehaving. There were police who were paid to catch bank robbers. There were jails to hold the criminals, but there was NO Boogie Man! He was just a make-believe character who was invented to frighten children to keep them in line.

Stinky smiled. He must have understood. He said, "I see what you mean! But, all the big people where I go to church believe in the devil, and they can't all be wrong. Maybe the devil *is* real and the Boogie Man is *not* real.

Stinky's new confidant told him of the time when thousands of Spaniards believed that the world was flat. They would not travel too far from home because they believed that they would fall off the world and never come home again. They were afraid. They knew that the world was flat, and they were afraid to travel to the edge.

Stinky said that he had heard that story in school. He said he knew that the world was round, even though so many believed it to be flat. The therapist told Stinky that if all those people could be wrong about the shape of the world, then so could all the big people that he knew be wrong about the devil. It was a story that people made to control the behavior of others. If you can convince people to be afraid of something, then you can control their behavior. If you want people to stay around home, then you tell them that the world is flat and they will fall off and never come back if they go too far from home. No one wants to fall off the world and never come back, so they will stay home and not travel too far even when they are not being watched. It works, and Stinky could begin to see the point.

This was not enough though, for now Stinky was afraid for the therapist. He said, "You had better be careful too or the devil might hear you talk this way about him, and he might come and get you too!" At this point, the therapist became aggressive. He said, "If you learn where the devil is and how to get a message to him, tell him to come to see me. I'll be happy to scold him for scaring a nice little boy like you. Just tell him where I am and that I'm waiting to meet him whenever he's ready!" Stinky smiled but did not reply.

The day continued and the therapist spent an hour with Stinky's aunt in therapy while he waited in the lobby. It was not to be known for a couple of weeks, but Stinky met a nice lady in the waiting room who asked him why he was visiting the mental health center. He told the lady of his fear of the creature that lived under the soil and of his talk with the doctor down the hall. He told the lady how the doctor did not believe in the devil and how he challenged the devil to come to see him and that he doctor would punch him in the nose for scaring the little boy.

That next week, the lady from the waiting room went to see the preacher and told him how the therapist did not believe in the devil and how he had told the little boy in the waiting room that there was no such thing. The preacher told the woman that he could understand, for "all psychologists are atheists." The woman came back to see the therapist for further treatment and told him what she had told the preacher and what he had said about therapists. She said what she told him must have upset him, for the very next Sunday, the preacher gave a sermon on how his people will not need therapists if they will just read their Bibles. He said that the Bible holds all the answers for humanity and that people need do nothing more than to read their Bibles for direction.

The lady was confused. She asked, "Are you supposed to question what I believe? Are you supposed to argue with what I've been taught for all these years? Is it right to question what you believe?" The therapist told the lady that he believed that his job was to challenge those attitudes and beliefs that disturbed his clients. If one's attitudes and beliefs are in one's best interest, then one feels good. When your beliefs cause you to shake, to lose sleep and to be very fearful, then you might conclude that your beliefs are not in your best interest. You might want to choose attitudes and beliefs that serve you better. You might want to change your beliefs to those that allow you to enjoy life and to be relatively calm and at peace with the world. If your belief in the flatness of the world keeps you from going to places you might like to visit, then you might want to give up your limiting beliefs and travel as you wish. If your belief of the devil keeps you immobilized and in the house and keeps you from enjoying life, then you might want to challenge that belief and ask yourself whether the belief makes any sense.

The human brain can believe truth or fiction, and to believe that Santa Claus flies through the air with reindeer might serve you well as a child, but may *not* serve you well as an adult. You can simply question your belief in the privacy of your own room and ask yourself if it is in your best interest to continue to believe what you now hold to be true.

There are better ways to teach young people like Stinky to be well behaved than by frightening them. We do not have to lie to young people to teach them to behave properly.

This young man learned to *fear* something rather than to *value* something. He learned that he could become "bad" by making mistakes. He learned to fear a creature that does not exist, and the negative became his focal point.

Don't lie to Stinky. Tell him about how life really is, and chances are he will make the right choices. Stinky does not want to be afraid and unhappy. Stinky wants to love and be loved. He wants to be taught the truth. He needs you to guide him. He will trust you and believe in what you tell him.

Be objective with Stinky. Tell him how things really are.

Food For Thought

- Are there adults in your life who have irrational (not in their best interest) fears such as Stinky? Please describe at least one of them.

- After reading this story, what could you tell him/her that might be helpful?

- Do you have an irrational fear comparable to Stinky? Is there something new that you could recommend to yourself, after reading this story, that might help you become more peaceful?

Fake It... Till You Make It!

Once upon a time, I was involved with a special project where children were sent who were "too ill mentally" to ever be returned to their parents and families. The children in this particular hospital did not follow directions nor comply with the requests and expectations of their parents. They were thought to be "too ill to benefit from therapy." The plan was to house them in a safe environment where they could not harm themselves or their family members. They were to live in a hospital setting for the rest of their lives.

From time to time there were professionals who thought they could help the children and they received permission from the hospital administration and the parents to experiment. The doctors and the researchers sincerely wanted to disprove the theory that "these children were too mentally ill to ever be helped."

No one was ever really successful. The children continued to be almost totally uncooperative with their peers and with the adults who looked after them at the hospital. For example, if asked to sleep in their beds, the children would sleep under them, or in the bathroom, or in the hall. If asked to eat with a spoon, they would eat with their hands. If asked to urinate in the toilet, they would urinate everywhere but in the toilet. They seemed to work hard at being uncooperative.

One day a psychologist came to the hospital. He wanted to help the children and he believed he knew how. The psychologist received permission to "try it his way" for a while. He bought hundreds of red poker chips and he designed a very specific list of behavioral expectations for the children. He told the children that *if* they behaved as expected they could *earn* a red chip. He said that *if* they slept in their assigned beds at night, they would earn one chip. If they awoke in the morning when called they could earn another chip. If they got dressed before coming to breakfast in the morning they could earn another chip. If they ate with their spoon, instead of their hands, they could earn a chip. The children were *not* interested in this new game. They had no incentive to cooperate.

So, the psychologist took away the children's right to watch television. He took away their right to play in the yard. He took away their snacks and their desserts after dinner. He took away all their treats and their privileges. He took away all the activities the children liked.

He explained that from this point forward, the children would have to *earn* the privilege to do what *they* wanted by first doing what *he* expected. There was increased grumbling on the part of the children. They wanted what they wanted, when they wanted it! They were angry and upset when they didn't get what *they* wanted. We are all like that from time to time, I suppose.

It was not long before one of the children wanted a candy bar. It was explained that he could have the candy bar when he earned 2 red chips. The young boy had no chips. The doctor explained that he could earn one by eating his next meal with his spoon...by sleeping in his bed tonight...by taking a shower before he went to bed...by not hitting another patient for the rest of the day. The young boy fussed, but he complied with the doctor's wishes long enough to earn 2 chips so that he could purchase the candy bar. The plan had begun to work!

It didn't happen overnight, but soon more and more children were doing what the adults expected in order to earn red chips to exchange for the things that they wanted at the hospital. More and more children began to act as directed. They began to act as their adult models expected. They began to behave as though they were not mentally ill. They stopped hitting and spitting on each other...they slept in their own beds at night...they urinated in toilets and not in the halls...they took showers each day...they agreed to dress in normally expected clothing for their day's activities...they went to class when asked...and they complained significantly less than before. Their behavior was changing!

There are always people who seemingly don't want others to be successful and there were those same people in this case. They said that the children were changing their behavior, but they weren't being cooperative because *they* wanted to be cooperative. They said that the children still wanted to misbehave even though they were "acting" cooperative. The skeptics charged the new psychologist with simply getting the children to "act normal." The doctor had his own belief: that it was acceptable if the children were only "acting" normal, because if they continued to "act" normal, they would someday grow to believe that this "acting" was indeed the right and personally acceptable way to behave. Someday the children would behave cooperatively because they believed that it was right and in their best interest to do so.

Within one year, some of the children were returned to their families. They were behaving, as a normal child would be expected to behave. Was it an "act" or not? There was much discussion on that topic.

Do you act cooperative because you *want* to, or because it is in your best interest, or because someone has raised you on red poker chips? You may answer those questions for yourself, if you like.

Let's move on. Not too long ago, administratively and clinically, I managed a chemical dependency treatment center for children between the ages of 12 and 18. By the time the children/druggies came to the Center for help they not only had a drug-abusing habit, they were very uncooperative with their parents, siblings, school personnel, religious leaders, law enforcement, and neighbors. Their lives seemed to be out of control and self-destructive, except to the young druggies themselves. They insisted, "They were doing what *they* wanted to be doing!" They said time and time again, "I want what I want when I want it!"

The behavior of the young druggies reminded me very much of the behavior of many of the children in the State Hospital. They were seemingly out of control…almost totally uncooperative…and demanding what *they* wanted when *they* wanted it.

The adolescents entered the drug program kicking and screaming. They "…didn't have a problem and they didn't want help!" Their message was clear. One young boy spit on his mother on the day of admission and told her he never wanted to see her again. He "…hoped she'd die, and soon!" One girl screamed at her mother, called her a "bitch" and said she'd kill her if she ever saw her again. The children were very abusive to their parents, even though there was usually no evidence that their parents had been abusive to them. How did the children get that way?

In some cases, the answers were simple. The boys and girls *practiced* a new set of behaviors or life-style until it became the acceptable life-style. They *acted* or *pretended to be* druggies, and eventually they made it!

I remember the first time I smoked a cigarette. My drama coach smoked when I was in high school and I wanted to be just like him. He smoked Camel cigarettes so I bought some. I lit one and inhaled deeply like he did. You're right! My eyes watered, I felt dizzy and nauseated, and coughed. I practiced in private so others would not see that I was not an accomplished smoker. I practiced and practiced and soon I could smoke and "be cool" like Mr. Jenkins. I had trained myself to be a smoker. I even trained my body to believe that it *needed* and *wanted* me to smoke on a regular basis.

It is possible for me to *drastically* change my behavior. I changed so very well from being a non-smoker to a smoker that several years later it was hard to give up the habit. I had to practice and practice, once again, to change back to a non-smoker. But, I did it and that is the point—I can change my behavior when I want to.

The boys and girls in the chemical dependency rehabilitation program changed their behavior also. Hundreds of angry, resentful, depressed, self-hating, uncooperative, snarling, biting, spitting, drug-abusing young people *reversed* their behaviors when they began to admit that their self-destructive acts were not in their own best interest. They were not self-destructive, angry, resentful, self-hating children when they were born. They *practiced* being that way! Adults did not make them that way.

You cannot be made to hate if you don't want to hate. That is the choice of each human being. We can choose to love or hate others, and ourselves. There are lots of choices about lots of things in the world.

Changing is not an easy process. Human beings cannot simply decide to be different and everything changes. First we have to admit that change would be in our own best interest. We have to have a reason to change. Many of us demand that *others* change so that *we* can feel better, rather than looking for ways in which *we* can make the situation or relationship more workable or pleasant ourselves. We tend to "point the finger" away from ourselves and toward someone or something external to ourselves.

I suggest that we look *within* ourselves to see what it is that "I" can do to help make this a better world in which to live, rather than blame others and wait for others to act first.

I met a young woman who looked sad and acted angry. I wanted to be her friend but she acted like she would rather not have me near her. In fact, she acted as if she would rather not have anyone relate to her. One day I asked her why she seldom smiled or acted friendly. She said something I will never forget...she said, "If I showed people my good side they will only take advantage of me!" She saw no reason to smile. How must she feel *inside*? I can only assume that she feels the same as she looks...sad and angry.

She found fault in others. She appeared to find little joy and happiness in life, and she sounded as if she thinks *other people* and *other things* are responsible for the way she feels. I'd like to tell her that she has options and choices. In fact, she has lots of options. I attempted to tell her that *if* she would relate in a friendly manner to me, I would very much like to be her friend. She was not impressed. She did not want to talk about that subject with me. She practiced being unhappy and angry for a long time and so she was skillful in producing these feelings for herself.

The young druggies that I treated were also well practiced in feeling miserable. They "felt like hell" most of the time and they blamed their boyfriends, girlfriends, mothers, fathers, brothers, sisters, teachers, ministers, and so on. But, sometimes, the young people would hear and understand. Something that we'd say or do would get through to them. They would actually begin to understand that *they* had choices about how *they felt* and about how others treated them. They thought adults didn't care about what happened to them. We'd tell them and show them that *we cared*. They thought and acted as if adults could not be trusted. We showed them that when we said something we meant it and we did what we said we'd do. They thought that all adults would like to get what they want. We told them the *facts*, to the best of our ability. They thought that adults are only out for themselves. We told them and showed them that we needed each other and that life is a team project. They began to trust us, work with us, and gain the insight that it matters what each of us does. They also grew to agree with me that it is fun, and personally rewarding, to have a *friend* and to be *loved*.

If we are not emotionally disturbed or mentally ill, don't most of us want to have a real friend and to be loved? Of course we do! We want to fit in. We want the people around us to approve of us. We want to be loved.

The young druggies adopted a <u>miserable</u> set of attitudes regarding themselves and their lives. Then they lived them as though they were the only ones that could ever be followed. They said, "I behaved rotten, therefore I am rotten!" They made this statement with all the conviction they could muster. It was difficult to break through their armor and to introduce the notion of human fallibility.

Then came the idea that humans are somehow responsible for human emotion. We make <u>ourselves</u> happy or sad. I am the one who suffers the most from my unhappiness and anger. Therefore, I don't want to suffer anymore than I have to. It is my personal *choice* to be sad and miserable! I can *choose* to be happy, friendly, pleasant, kind, cooperative, peaceful, and gentle if I want to. Can't I?

My young druggie clients began to *choose* to be friendly, gentle, peaceful, cooperative, calm, and happy. They really did! The majority of them changed so drastically in a year and a half of treatment that their parents, ministers, grandparents, teachers and neighbors were amazed.

Human beings are *powerful* creatures! We can do great and wonderful things with our lives. We are capable of *change* whenever we decide to get *honest* with ourselves.

The first step the young people took is called *insight*. They learned some new information...a light went on...they took some friendly advice...they thought about themselves and their plight honestly and objectively. They said, "Maybe, just maybe, Dr. Brown is accurate. Maybe I *am* responsible for my miserable life and the miserable way that I feel. Maybe if I did what he is suggesting…maybe I could make a difference in my life…just maybe."

Many of the teenagers liked the idea of living "one day at a time." Making an effort to change a personal behavior for a day was far less threatening than changing for the "rest of my life." One girl thought that even "a day" was too difficult a goal for her, so we made success even more possible to achieve. She said, "one moment at a time." She found success with this new attitude.

For these recovering druggies, the *intellectual insight* that "I am at least partially responsible for my sad state of affairs," was important for them to understand. Being responsible for my thinking and attitudes provides hope and gives a new sense of power because, it means, when I change *what* I *think*, my feelings and behavior will also change. I feel and act the way I do because of the *thoughts* I think.

The young woman in my story does not have to be angry, sad and miserable. She can learn to think differently. She now *thinks* that people will take advantage of her if she smiles, acts friendly, and is cooperative. She could *think* instead that people, like her mother, want very much to be her friend, enjoy a positive relationship with her, and enjoy her company. She *thinks* that it is unfair and awful that her father and mother got divorced and she cannot be happy without them the way they used to be. She could choose to *think* that the world is not always fair. She could think both her mother and father are happier apart than they were living with each other, and she could choose to enjoy their new happiness. She could choose to deal with the *present* rather than with the past, and enjoy the relative peace of the moment.

She does not have to feel miserable at this moment because she's not getting everything she'd like to have! She can ask herself the following question? What is it that I would have to tell myself *right now* to make myself feel better than I presently do? Then, she could tell herself, whatever is necessary, to get on with her happier life! Example? Life just doesn't always give me what I want. If life gives me a bag of lemons, I could choose to make some lemonade. Life seems to be spelled "HASSLE" from time to time. It isn't the hassle I *get that's important*. It's what I *do* with the hassle that's really important. Life can be one damn thing after another. Counting how many "damn things" I get is not as important as what I do about them and how I handle them. I have some choices, you know!

When life does not give her what she very much wants, she can *choose* to whine about it, or accept that "it" happened. It wasn't what she wanted, but she can stand it, and move on. Perhaps the supposed problem may even be a *window of opportunity* that cannot be seen clearly at the moment...

Human beings have *choices* about how they emotionally feel because they have *choices* about what they *think* about themselves and their environment. Humans feel the way they do because of the thoughts they think.

Most of the teenagers I worked with understood this insight eventually. They fought tooth and nail not to change...they seemed to be willing to do almost anything to keep their misery, hatred, and resistance to change. They believed that *other* people and *other* things were responsible for their upset, period! Once they understood how their thinking and attitudes played a vital role in their emotional lives and how they behaved, they were willing to start making some changes. Once they saw that they were individually responsible for their miserable state, they started to agree, "they were not going to continue to punish themselves as they had once learned to do."

These druggie children needed to care about themselves as individuals. They seemed to enjoy the new idea that they are VFHB's (valuable, fallible, human beings). They liked the way that new attitude felt.

They also had to believe they were worth the effort. They had to *like* themselves before they could start treating themselves well. The druggies treated themselves poorly because they hated themselves for the way they had behaved in their past. How else could they treat themselves as they did?

If the young lady in this story really liked *herself,* she would not alienate herself from her parents. She might even take some advice from them. She might even appreciate their efforts to befriend her. She might even invite her mother over for lunch and find out how good it feels to have a mother who loves her. It is amazing to me how human beings will work so very hard to keep loving people away from them.

This particular young woman has a mother who loves her dearly; who has remained her friend no matter what her daughter has done. The mother sends her support money; accompanied her to the delivery room when others were too afraid to go with her; makes sure that she has the items necessary to be a new mother; supplies clothing and furniture for the new baby; listens to her tears in the middle of the night when she calls on the phone; and is always available for requested support. However, it you were to watch when the mother does something kind for her daughter, you would see the daughter behave as though a stranger were doing something irritating to her. It seems to make no rational sense.

Why would a young woman, with a new baby, and no partner, push away a loving mother? It is a *learned*, self-defeating *attitude* that the girl has practiced for a long time. She learned to think about her mother as someone who does not have her best interest at heart. She was someone to avoid, someone to get around, and someone who was only there to stop her from having "fun." She practiced this thinking long enough to believe it. She got plenty of support from her friends because in some sub-cultures it is "popular" to find one's parents offensive.

What would ever motivate the girl to change? Her life is becoming more and more uncomfortable, unmanageable and painful. Her boyfriend, with whom she had a baby, wants her to "get out" of their apartment. He is "tired of the responsibility of caring for her and their baby."

Rather than get angry with the boyfriend at this point, let's concentrate on the less-fortunate young woman and the baby. She needs to survive somehow with her child. She needs to care enough about herself, which she has not done for several years. She needs to clean herself up, get help caring for the baby, and get a job to support the two of them. Will that be "easy?" No, but it is possible!

The first required change is in *attitude*. The young mother would do well to consider that she and her baby are worth the effort that she needs to make in order to save the two of them. She needs to *pretend* that they are worth the effort even if she does not really believe it. She probably will not believe it when she first thinks about it. She probably will not believe it when first she thinks the thought. She must *fake it...till she makes it.*

"Fake It...Till You Make It," was one of our most popular and important phrases in drug treatment with the 400 children and families we served. It does not feel "right" to attempt something different than what you've been used to. Imagine the girl in the story calling her mother and saying, "I miss you and would love to visit with you. I am going to make a nice lunch for you this Thursday at noon. I'll clean my apartment, put on a pretty dress and a smile and make our time together a special one. Please join me." The mother and the daughter would both be uncomfortable and nervous because that is not typical behavior for either of them. But, it just might feel very good for both of them afterwards. I bet it would!

The first time we do something that we are unaccustomed to doing; we have to be somewhat uncomfortable. It is human and natural to feel that way. But, the more we *practice* being kind, appreciative, loving and gentle, the easier it becomes. Someone said that with practice we could do almost anything.

I have seen *practice* work "miracles" in the State Hospital with children, in intensive drug rehabs with adolescents and their parents, and in mental health centers with people of all ages. Human beings who were willing to *fake it…till they make it,* made it!

What's the risk? What did the young woman in the story risk? She risks becoming less miserable…gaining one or two close, trusted friends…feeling calmer, more peaceful and more content. The risk is experiencing the world as an enjoyable place.

A person can start by repeating the following thoughts (again and again). And, while saying the words, like a great actor or actress might say them, *pretend* that *you really want to believe what you are saying.*

- I am a valuable human being.

- I am a fallible human being.

- I deserve to be happy and healthy.

- I am far more capable than I presently believe.

- I am responsible for my happiness.

- I want to be happier, calmer and more peaceful.

- I am going to start today to *act* cooperative, appreciative, loving, kind, and gentle, especially toward those who love me and care about me.

- I am not too proud to ask for help.

- I will keep *my* best interest in mind at all times.

- I am going to *fake it, till I make it*, because ***I am worth it!***

Food For Thought

- It is not uncommon to see a person behave in a certain manner and then say, "That's just the way I am…I've always done it that way. There doesn't seem to be much I can do about it. It seems too uncomfortable, or phony, to act differently." They have a habit of behaving in a certain manner and believe they were born doing it that way. Have you ever said the very same thing to yourself? Were you aware that "faking it till you make it" is useful advice?

- Do you remember faking it till you made it? What were the circumstances?
- If this is a new idea for you, how might you put the idea to use in your life?

Candy

It was a beautiful, sunny and warm day on the west coast of Florida. The temperature was in the eighties and the humidity was low. It was simply a pleasure to be alive. It was hard to imagine there were unhappy people in the world on a day such as this. I had a peaceful morning at the office with some paperwork to complete and no student problems to resolve.

When my lunch hour arrived, I climbed into my yellow, Jaguar XKE convertible and headed west for the short drive over the causeway to the beach along the Gulf of Mexico. The top was down on the car, the sun was warm, and the scenery could not have been more beautiful. I could smell the salt air as I drove through downtown toward the beach. The roads were crowded with tourists, both in their cars and walking, and everywhere I looked I saw people rushing off to someplace important. As I drove over the causeway to the beach I once again felt transformed into a special feeling human being. It was like closing my eyes and imagining that I was driving into paradise. There was blue-green water on both sides of the causeway, dotted with tall, green palm trees, and bushes covered with red and yellow flowers were everywhere. The scene was right out of Travel and Leisure Magazine.

Soon I was leaving the beach highway and pulling into a parking spot along the beach. I dropped some coins into a parking meter, left my shoes and socks on the floor of the E-type, hung my tie over the rearview mirror and was off across the hot sand to the water. What a wonderful feeling! The air was so very fresh, the breeze was gentle, the people on the beach were relaxing and becoming tanner by the minute, and I was at peace with the world. There seemed, for this brief period of time, to not be any significant cares in the world. All seemed at rest. Even the gulf was lapping at the shore with a gentle motion. I felt as if I had been transformed from the real world onto a new planet. It was a very peaceful experience indeed.

I recall walking along the beach for almost an hour, just enjoying the many birds in flight, the little sand crabs digging quickly out of sight as I approached, and the young and not-so-young people soaking up the warm rays of the sun. I felt renewed with energy as I walked, and I thought how I wanted everyone to have this peaceful experience.

I admit thinking that I wanted to spend the rest of my day right here on the beach, or perhaps even the rest of my life. Yet, it was time to return to the office and to respond to calls from school personnel throughout the county who had students in need of help. I had moved to Florida just six months earlier to take a position as a school psychologist.

It was a challenging and yet frustrating position for me to fill because I cared a great deal about the young people. I had the talent and skills they could utilize in resolving their personal conflicts, yet just the title of "psychologist" was enough to send parents and students alike, running away from me. I meet people even today who believe that I know what they are thinking before they utter a word. People accuse me of reading their minds. I wonder where they think I get that magical ability? I cannot read minds any better than they can.

I also meet people everyday that believe that I spent all my time analyzing others, whether they want me to or not. Even more humorous to me is the notion that I can analyze them without them speaking to me.

Some students and parents even say that I scare them because I am a psychologist. These are some of the things that I think about when I am not walking along the Gulf of Mexico, and when I get off on tangents about how to make the rest of the world happier and more content.

Anyway, it was time to turn left into the parking lot in front of my office and to focus my attention on our student population. As I entered the front door of the building, my secretary said, "Doc, you better call the principal at Eastwood High School right away! He needs your help!" I called Mr. Evans and learned that he had a student in his office that wanted to talk with me.

I left the building and walked the short distance to the high school. As I entered the principal's office, I noticed the young woman that wanted help. She was sitting next to the door, her head in her hands, with tears rolling down her cheeks.

Mr. Evans told me about Candy and her attempt to physically harm herself. She was upset about her relationship with her parents. I asked to be able to talk with Candy alone. The principal gave us his office and left. I asked Candy to tell me what was happening to her. She said something to me that I will never forget. "Dr. Brown, my parents can make me upset whenever they want to, and keep me that way for as long as they want!" She said that she was "sick of them," and wanted to "end her life." I was naturally concerned about what she said, but excited at the same time. How could I be excited about what Candy told me? I knew that her parents could not upset her, and they could not keep her upset for as long as they might choose. I knew that for a fact. They did not have that power over her. If what Candy reported was indeed factual, then you and I would simply be puppets that could be turned on and off, emotionally, by others, and we would have no self-control. This is not the case at all. We are not simply puppets under the emotional control of other people.

Now my energy would be spent teaching Candy to think factually and realistically about who she is and what she can really do. I was excited about this new relationship because I do not want young people, or any people for that matter, believing they are out of control regarding their emotional lives. I looked at Candy and told her I could help her! I said, "I know that you might not believe what I am about to tell you, but I can help you because I know that your parents do not have the power over you that you think they do, and I want to teach you how to care for yourself so you do not have to suffer as you have been." I could see by Candy's reaction she did not believe what I just told her; however, she did agree to sit still long enough to hear me out.

We have been taught beliefs that are not factual and then act as if they are. It is possible to believe that all spiders are dangerous, even though they are not. Then when one is spotted, we feel afraid though there is, in fact, nothing to fear. I believe it is important to know what and who is able to create fear in us. Is the spider the force that creates fear in us, or is fear the result of our attitudes and beliefs? It is really the fault of our attitudes and beliefs, isn't it? If we see a picture of a spider and feel fear, would we blame the picture? Ink on a sheet of paper does not have the power to cause fear in a human being. When I think scary thoughts about a spider picture, or imagine a spider crawling on me, I scare myself with the thoughts. It is my *thought* about the spider that causes the fear and not the ink, paper or image of the spider.

For the same reason, one person cannot make another person feel angry when he chooses. When I think anger-producing thoughts, then I feel anger. I control what I think, not others.

This was not easy for Candy to understand at first. Almost everything she was taught since she was born led her to believe that other people and other things cause her to feel the way she does.

Candy remembered when she was a little girl, her mother saying she had hurt her feelings by doing something her mother did not like. When Candy got her dress soiled, her mother would say, "You make Mommy feel bad when you get your dress dirty!" Candy might stop to visit with a friend on the way home from school and arrive home later than expected. Her mother would say, "You worried me when you did not come home from school on time!"

I think her mother meant well. She taught her daughter what she believed to be true. Her mother believed that Candy was the cause of her hurt feelings, and the cause of her worry, and she told her so.

The fact is that Candy's soiled dress cannot, and did not cause her mother's upset feelings. It was not the soiled dress, nor Candy, that was responsible for the mother's discomfort. Her mother may have believed that her little girl should do as she asked, and when Candy soiled her dress her mother was disappointed. She did not get the results she wanted. Her mother expected her daughter's dress to remain clean. When she got a typical little girl with a soiled dress, she was disappointed and perhaps even angry. She didn't get what she wanted. The belief that her little girl should absolutely not get dirt on her dress was the upsetting factor, not the dirty dress. Candy didn't know that. She loved and believed her mother. If her mother said she got her dress dirty, and hurt her mother's feelings, then most likely she did. Candy was learning to believe that she could hurt her mother's feelings even though it was not possible to do so.

When Candy forgot to be a responsible little girl and did not arrive home on time, her mother would worry. Her mother likely learned that "a good mother worries about her children," and, "children are a worry to their parents," and even, "if a mother worries about her children it will help." Well, it is possible for Candy to come home late from school and her mother not to have worried about her. Mom has an alternative to worry. What is it? Her mother might have remembered that she gave Candy permission to stop for a visit with her girlfriend on her way home. Her mother could walk to her friends to look for her, or make some phone calls. Her mother could call the school to see if someone had seen Candy after school. Her mother could remember that Candy found her way home lots of times previous to this, and is likely to come home safely tonight.

When life does not go as we plan or expect, we tend to imagine the worst happening, and it almost never does.

Anyway, Candy learned that she controlled the way her mother felt. She learned that she could drive her teachers up the wall if she wanted. She learned that she could give her dad a headache when he came home from work. She learned that she could drive her sister crazy. She had lots of emotional power at a very young age. The problem was, Candy believed her parents had the same power over her. They can make her angry whenever they want, and keep her that way for as long as they choose. This is make-believe-power that only seems to be real!

Candy, because of her early childhood education, was willing to believe that her parents had this ability. So, when her parents gave her a reason to make herself angry, she did as they expected. When they did what was required for Candy to be upset for days, Candy kept herself upset for days. The beliefs that Candy was using to upset herself were old and well learned. The excitement was that Candy could change! She could learn new response to old parental behaviors.

Candy controls what she thinks, not her parents. Candy's attitudes and beliefs control her emotions, not her parents'. Candy is in charge of Candy. She just doesn't know it yet.

Imagine believing that you are in prison and cannot escape, but the next day finding the key to your cell in your own pocket. The path to freedom is free for the taking. That is what Candy was about to find out.

If you ever believed that someone else controlled your emotional life when you would rather they didn't have the power, then you also have something to gain from what Candy was about to learn. It is fun for me to find someone who seems emotionally hopeless and to demonstrate they indeed have the ability to climb out of the hopelessness. Finding solutions to problems where we see only hopelessness is thrilling. Once we see we have the ability to erase hopelessness under one set of circumstances, we find it easier to see the light at the end of the tunnel next time.

The poem, "I Am Your Master," explains, "Our Master" is our own attitudes and beliefs, not something external to us. Our thoughts can make us happy, they can make us sad, they can be the love we share with others, or create the hatred by which we hurt others. My thoughts are the vehicles used on the Florida beach to transport myself to paradise. There are others complaining on the very same beach that it is too hot, there is nothing to do, or wishing they were some place nicer.

Candy was a willing subject because she felt lousy. She felt that way for a long time. She could not see a healthy way out of the misery, only that of harming herself. I wanted to offer her an alternative! Is it possible that a significant portion of our suffering is self-imposed?

We don't suffer like this because we want to, or because we are sick. We upset ourselves the way we do because we have had good, if not great, role models. The "soaps" are popular teachers of how others create our sadness, anger, hatred and fears. Our best and favorite teachers taught us that we controlled their emotional lives, and we theirs.

There is little good to come from blaming them. Other people only teach us to think and believe as they do. We cannot expect more from them. If they had known better they would have been different role models. They were the role models they knew how to be.

One day Candy came home late from school. She was not doing anything that she ought to be ashamed of, but she was indeed late to help her mother with the dinner chores. By the time Candy arrived home, her mother was angry. When Candy entered the kitchen door, her mother unloaded her anger on her. In the process of yelling at Candy for this lateness and others, she said, "You are nothing but a whore!" Those were strong words to hear with strong meanings attached. Candy rushed to her room and slammed the door. She did not come out for supper, and stayed in her room until it was time to come out for school the next day.

When Candy saw me at school the next day she told me what her mother had done. She told me how she went to her room and did not come out that evening. She said that it was her mother's fault and it was her mother who ruined the evening.

I had to agree that if Candy's mother called her a whore, it would not be fun and might be a shock. I could not agree that it was her mother who "hurt her feelings" and "spoiled the evening." In fact, when I asked Candy's mother to come in to talk with me, she said that she never for a moment thought that her daughter was a whore, or that she ought to spend any time in her room for what she had done. She said she wanted her daughter to be home on time to help her prepare dinner. Her mother had a very busy day at her job and really wanted her daughter's help. When her mother did not get what she wanted that afternoon, she made herself especially angry with all her thoughts about what she wanted and didn't get. She wanted her daughter to do what she wanted her to do! By the time Candy arrived home, her mother was saying things she did not mean. Her mom had plenty of time to upset herself waiting for her daughter.

What happened had happened, and I wanted Candy to know that she also had a <u>choice</u> about how to behave. She could have asked her mother how she could help at the late hour. She could have offered to wash the dishes after dinner to make up for her lateness. Candy knew she was not a whore, so why send herself to her room for something she was not.

We've all learned such intense emotional reactions to some words and phrases. If Candy's mother called her a "tennis shoe," she would most likely have laughed. Candy never learned to be angry when called a tennis shoe. She surely learned to upset herself when called a whore! Who upsets whom? Do you see my point? Do you understand you really do have an alternative? Do you understand you do have control over what you feel, emotionally? I wanted Candy to understand. I wanted her to understand her mother was angry. It is easy for us to take ownership of someone else's upset, and make ourselves upset at the same time. We, however, have a choice. We don't have to be angry just because someone else invites us. Does that sound strange? Does it sound strange to hear that when Candy walked into the house and her mother invited her to be angry, she had choices? Candy was angry long after her mother calmed down and relaxed in front of the television for the evening.

Candy's mother invited her daughter to join her in her angry mood. She gave her a good reason with her choice of words, and she used a higher volume voice to send her the message. Most of us have learned to feel insulted in that particular situation. Candy was no exception.

Candy's mom set the stage for Candy's potential academy award performance. When Candy saw the stage all prepared for her, she hopped right on it and did her best to receive a nomination. What if Madonna gave an outstanding performance one evening in concert and then blamed her parents for making her do it? Who was indeed performing? Who was singing? Who was making who do what? I believe that you are getting the message.

Close your eyes for a moment. Imagine one of the worst things that ever happened to you in your life. Imagine it being as awful as it was. Imagine the original people in the scene. Imagine them saying what they did. See yourself in the picture. Feel the way you felt when the situation was actually taking place. Imagine that nothing changed. Notice that you cannot change them still. What is the one thing that you can change? Allow the other people to do what they did. Allow them to say what they said. What is the one thing you can change to help you feel better almost instantly?

If you change the way you think about the people, what they are doing and saying, then you will come away from the memory feeling significantly different. Its not actually what they said or did that caused your upset, rather how you evaluated their behavior.

Sometimes we don't like what we see or hear from others. We prefer they talk or act differently. But, they talk, or behave, as they prefer, instead. Consider a past situation. Make yourself think differently about what happened to you. Make yourself look differently at the situation. If you thought he stabbed you in the back, take another look at the situation. Did you get stabbed in the back, or did he do something the way he wanted, and not as you wanted? It makes a difference.

What's the difference? What's the difference what Candy thinks? The difference is almost everything! If she thinks her mother stabbed her in the back for being late, she feels rotten. If she remembered that she promised to be home right after school to help her mother prepare dinner for her friends and family, and she was late, she might decide to apologize and get busy helping her. The benefit of thinking differently is that we feel less miserable. We recognize that our emotional reactions are indeed ours. We take responsibility for them. We own our own reactions. We utilize our choices, one being feeling less miserable.

When we think for ourselves, and don't just react through habit, we have increased personal power over anger, hate, fear, sadness, depression, contentment and happiness. Those are enough reasons to change some of our attitudes and beliefs. I have never enjoyed feeling badly, have you?

Candy was a high school student who had suffered significantly in the last several years. She didn't want to, but she believed that others were responsible for her unhappiness. She believed she had to get what she wanted from others. She believed others had to behave, as she wanted. I told her that she had the right and ability to upset herself whenever she didn't get what she wanted. She also had the right to change her thinking about her life.

She didn't like being called names by her mother. She loves her mother and she wants her mother to love her. She wants her mother to respect her. Sometimes her mother is tired, hungry, or frustrated with life. Sometimes her mother does not behave like Candy prefers. But, it is only a preference of Candy's. Candy does not have to get what she wants to be relatively calm. Candy is experienced enough to recognize anger in her mother and not demand that her mother treat her gently and kindly at that moment. Candy admitted that. When Candy wants one mood from her mother, and gets yet another, Candy can chose to walk softly and wait till her mother's mood changes. Candy could even offer her mother a sincere apology for her lateness, along with a hug and a smile.

I might refuse to give a Popsicle to a child when asked, but I am not responsible for the tears that follow. I may have to stop for a red light when I am late for a meeting, but I can chose how to think, and therefore feel, while waiting for the light to change. I have some significant choices. I have lots of choices!

Candy was listening to me, but she appeared not to believe. She accused me of being some kind of machine that never felt anything. She suggested that perhaps I never felt anything. I told her that I could get angry if I wanted to, and sometimes I did out of old habit. I have feelings like others. I just don't want her to go to her room angry and spend the night there if she would rather be somewhere else. It might be nice if next time she were in her room feeling upset, she could insightfully remember that she did not "have to" be there. She could remind herself to redefine how she got there, and who is responsible for her being there. She might just end her suffering earlier than before. That would be an improvement!

Often, it's simply a matter of degree, rather than feeling "perfectly" happy or "perfectly" upset. Practice leads to improvement.

Candy said she hopes each time her mother gets upset it will never happen again. The next time her mother is upset, Candy acts surprised and suffers all over again. Yes, Candy's mother could change. But, Candy is more in a position to change herself than change her mother. She will be more successful changing herself.

Candy could have more realistic expectations about her mother, and feel less threatened at the same time. Candy can expect that when she does not do what her mother asks, her mother will respond with anger toward her. If Candy realized the connection, then she would not be so "surprised and shocked" when encountering her mother's anger. "When I don't do what I promised to do, my mother is going to react in an angry fashion," she could say to herself. "I promised to be home on time tonight and I am late. My mother is going to be upset with me when I enter the house!"

Candy could also remember that Dr. Brown said, "Your mother is not responsible for how <u>you</u> feel. <u>You</u> are! Make an effort to comply with your mother's wishes and save yourself the hassle. That way you can <u>add</u> to the harmony in your family. In this case, <u>you</u> were in error in the first place. You didn't keep <u>your</u> promise and then acted surprised when your mother was upset. You could have predicted her reaction. You are not unintelligent in these matters!"

Reeducation does not come without practice. Our early education did not come without practice, sweat and lots of tears. The new education is not going to come without practice, sweat and perhaps some tears either. But, <u>it is possible to change</u>, that's the good news!

I am able to watch television wherein people are upset, crying, sad, or angry. I don't feel the way they do. I can watch others be upset and not feel the same. It is possible to see others upset and not experience their feelings myself. It is possible for Candy's mother to be upset, and Candy, remain calm. It <u>is</u> possible!

The most important person in this situation is Candy. She is asking for help. She wants to hurt less. She wants to understand herself better. Candy needs to know what her options are, and how to feel better without the use of drugs and other chemicals.

Candy has emotional alternatives, if and when she wants to practice them. She has been told that her emotions are <u>learned</u> reactions. Reeducation is possible for her. She knows the change requires practice. The new education will take as long as it takes, depending on her motivation to change. Each of us has varying motivational levels with varying intensities. Sometimes, the more we are hurting, the more we are motivated to change. That was certainly a factor in Candy's case.

She was learning to imagine a past situation and imagine how to think and behave differently in her mind. This is a safe and effective way in which to practice feeling and behaving differently next time a similar situation occurs. Imagination is a powerful tool in the reeducation process.

Candy seemed to understand that an invitation to argue did not have to be honored. She had the potential to learn to remain relatively calm when others around her are upset. The upset of others does not necessitate her being upset. Candy was learning that a fellow human being can't make her feel the way she chooses not to feel. Her mother cannot make her happy or sad, not really! We are not emotional puppets. We have lots of choices and alternatives, even when we think we do not.

I told Candy that when she gets to the point of thinking that she has run out of options, to remember that Dr. Brown says, "You do have choices. You are not aware of them at the moment, but you have some! If you can't think of them, ask me."

Please read the Little Golden Book, <u>The Little Engine That Could</u>. In fact, read it twice. The message is an important one for all of us. The big engine could not pull the cars over the hill because he thought, "They are too heavy a load." The Little Engine came along and pulled the cars over the mountain while chugging the thought, "I think I can…I think I can…I think I can." Those thoughts won't make all things possible, but they sure will free us to do more than we are presently doing. We will also feel less hopeless. Try it right now, "I think I can, I think I can, and really do think I can!"

What we <u>think</u> makes all the difference. Our thinking is our master. It can make us weak, or strong. It can make us happy or sad. It can allow us to try, or it can build a wall around us so we go nowhere. Thinking can reeducate us to be more the kind of person we want to be, or it can keep us down on ourselves and angry. It can make us love, or it can make us hate. It can create options and alternatives, or it can keep us in our bedrooms angry with others.

Candy was learning to think thoughts of herself and her mother that are more in her own best interest. She understands that <u>Candy</u> is responsible for <u>Candy's behavior</u>, not her mother.

I wish that I could introduce you to Candy today. She is a changed person. She suffers much less because she has taken responsibility for her own behavior. She has taken back the control that she once believed she had lost. The relationship between Candy and her mother has changed. Candy has been able to share what she is learning with her mother. That has been of benefit to both women.

Candy practices her newfound education daily, and I expect she'll only get better and better with time...

Food For Thought

- Who in your life has seemingly been able to upset you and keep you that way for longer than you wanted?

- What did he or she do to upset you?

- What specifically can you do today to become more in charge of your own emotional life?

- What do you have to think differently about yourself?

- What do you have to think differently about other people?

The Death Call

My first presentation of an introduction to Rational Thinking for senior high school psychology students went well. The majority of the students seemed to be listening and taking notes about what was being said. However, in the middle of the second class, I was accused of telling the students that they should not have <u>any</u> emotions. One girl in particular, accused me of sounding like a computer that acts and behaves without emotion, a machine that has no fun. At this point, I explained that what I was excited about was <u>controlling</u> my emotional life so that I suffered less, and was calm and even happier more often. I was not saying that we could do away with our emotions altogether. I told the students that I could get angry, or not get angry, as I choose. Since <u>my</u> brain controls <u>my</u> emotions, I have the ability to not be angry and upset if I choose not to be. I can learn emotional control just as I learn physical control.

The same girl spoke again. "OK," she said. "Let's suppose that everything is the same now in this room with the exception that we add a phone on your desk. The phone rings, you answer it, and a voice on the other end that you recognize and trust tells you that your wife has just died. My question, Dr. Brown, is <u>now</u> how are you going to feel? Your wife has just died and here you are telling us how great Rational Thinking and this new learning about emotions can be. What are <u>you</u> going to feel now?"

I must admit that this question was not included in the "teacher's guide." I hesitated a moment and then told class, "You are expecting me to say something special. Would you please tell me how you believe I <u>should</u> feel and how long I <u>should</u> feel that way?" The 34 students, without exception, thought I should feel bad, sad and/or unhappy for a period of time ranging from nine months to one year. The student who initially asked the question said, "All right, you know what we expect. So tell us how <u>you</u> would feel when you answered the phone!"

In reply I asked the class what their response would be if they noticed, after a moment or so, that I had a gentle smile on my face. Someone said, "You would have to have not loved your wife!" "You would be some kind of animal," said another. "You would not be human," came a third response. I then asked them to recall one of the most important ideas that I had shared with them a week before:

"We feel the way we do because of the thoughts we think. We can control what thoughts we want to think, and therefore feel the way we want to feel." I told the class of some beautiful moments regarding our wedding day, of some wonderful trips to the mountains and streams or southeast Arizona, of the birth of our child that we delivered together, of our first home in Florida and of some personally wonderful times we recently had together.

The class apparently forgot themselves for a moment, because the girl who had asked the death-feeling question now said, "Gee, those times sound very special to you and make me feel warm inside." At that moment a very important insight took place. Now the students could understand the soft smile on my face at a moment when they expected sorrow and pain. How could thoughts of beautiful moments with someone I love produce sadness? It was true I had the choice at the moment to think thoughts like, "She is gone and I will never see her again," or "I certainly am going to miss her." Those thoughts would surely lead to feelings of sadness. The <u>choice</u>, however, of which thoughts and feelings to have, is up to me.

I then insisted that the class hear one other admission. I told them I was not perfect, that I would die a fallible human being just as I was born, and therefore I would never completely master the use of Rational Thinking. While I could not be sure how I would react if and when I receive that "phone call," I could tell them now that through a practiced understanding of Rational Thinking I would be sad and depressed only as long as I decided to make myself sad and depressed.

That was not the last class period I spent with those students however. Some of them still meet with me individually on my visits to their school to share with me their work in rational emotional re-education. As an end to this personally exciting experience, I received a call from the mother of the girl that asked me to respond to the "death call." The mother reported, "Something wonderful had happened to the relationship between her and her daughter." "The two of us have fought for the past seventeen years and we have not had a very happy relationship. A couple of months ago my daughter came home, looked at me and said that she was never again going to make herself angry at me. You know, Dr. Brown, we have had a wonderful new relationship because she refuses to get angry with me and therefore I have a hard time staying angry with her. We really work out the problems together somehow now. I sure hope that you continue to do to my daughter whatever you have been doing these past nine months. She is a changed person...and I suppose I've changed a great deal also. Thank you!"

I told the girl's mother that her daughter had <u>learned</u> something about Rational Thinking and that she had made the effort to apply it to her personal life. I assured her that I had done nothing whatsoever <u>to</u> her daughter. It is up to <u>her</u> to do something to and for herself, I concluded. And, it seems that she is.

<u>Food For Thought</u>

- Some people say that death is a tragedy. Others have said it is a blessing. Sometimes death is celebrated. Other times death is mourned. What makes the difference?

- When deaths have occurred in your family or circle of friends, how have you defined them differently? What was different about the events?

- When you think about the people closest to you, how do you imagine their deaths will impact you? Is there a difference in how you define their inevitable deaths?

- Is there something sensible you can do <u>now</u> to better prepare <u>yourself</u> for these events in your life?

This Isn't Really Happening To Me!

They came into my office on Sunday afternoon to talk to me. They had talked to me almost two years ago when their daughter was twelve, now she is fourteen. They could not control her behavior when she was twelve and that had not changed. "She is, if anything, getting along with her brother somewhat better after two years of individual counseling, but everything else is just about the same or worse!" Her father said that he "wanted to knock her teeth out just last week!" The reason was that "she seldom talks to me, and when she does she uses such foul language and calls me such foul names that I just about cannot stand it! I would have punched her in the mouth but she is wearing several thousand dollars worth of braces that I had just purchased for her!"

Their daughter does not come home when she is asked. "Just a week ago, several boys in their late teens came to the house to see her. We did not know the boys and our daughter did not introduce them to us. It was 10 p.m. and she said that she just wanted to walk around the block with them." Her dad told her to be home in an hour. Thinking that she would probably not return home on time her dad told the four boys that he wanted them to make sure that his daughter was home in an hour. They agreed to have her home as expected.

Two hours later it was midnight and her father decided to go looking for his daughter. He could not find her but he found the home of one of the boys. He learned that his daughter was "down at the river with the other boys." He found the boys, blamed them for not having his daughter at home and told them to never be seen around his house again. He was "very angry at them."

How do we get this way? What was the daughter's responsibility? Where was she supposed to be and whose responsibility is it?

"She is very defiant when we ask her to do anything," her mother said. "She gets more and more hostile all the time! She seldom talks to me unless she wants something from me. She demands, rather than asks, and she gets furious if I say no. Recently I said no to her and she went into her bedroom and trashed it! She smashed and broke most of what was in there. She was really on a rampage! We asked her psychologist what we should do and he said that our daughter needed some love and understanding. So, we tried not to make a big deal of what she had done to her room. We just left it that way until she cleaned it herself...that was a long time later, however! Her anger and her manipulation are somewhat new these past few years but really I don't believe that it could be drug abuse!"

"So what do you think is behind your daughter's behavior? Why is she acting like this?" I asked.

"We really are not sure," said her father, "but we don't believe that it's drugs. The psychologist says that we need to love her more and be more understanding, but I am not sure how to be understanding of what she is doing, or how to love her more."

"Recently my wife and I went away for the weekend and left our daughter at home. When we came back on Sunday night we found the windshield on our second car had been smashed. We asked our daughter if she knew what happened and she said she had not seen the damage. We called the police and they were unable to determine what had happened. Several weeks later we learned that our daughter and her friend had spent the night together at our home. They wanted some cigarettes and could not buy their own. They knew I smoked and kept a carton under the seat of the car. They could not find the keys to the car so they smashed in the front window with a brick to get my cigarettes. When they got into the car they 'were so angry that they slashed the seats with a knife.' But I really do not think that drugs are involved!"

"So what do you think is behind your daughter's behavior...why do you think she would do such things? Is she perhaps insane, or could her insane behavior come from chemical abuse?" I asked.

Her dad went on to tell me how he found his 14-year-old daughter in the back seat of a car with three young men. "They had her undressed and they were playing with her," he said. I almost killed those boys! I wanted to kill them and something stopped me! I could not believe what they were doing to my daughter! As I attempted to stop them my daughter called me names that I seldom have heard. She said that I should go away and let her alone. She said that she knew what she was doing. She fought me, kicking and screaming, as I forced her into my car to take her home. The boys ran away the first chance they had and my daughter was furious with me. I hated those young men!"

How did we ever get this way, I asked myself. How do we look past what our children are doing and blame someone else? Is it that we have to blame ourselves when our children do not live up to our expectations? Is our children's behavior our fault?

"Yes, sure, my daughter has a beer now and then! Once she got a little drunk with some of her girlfriends at a party and we had to go and get her. That does not mean that she had a drug problem!" said her father. "You know kids will be kids and perhaps it is just a stage my daughter is going through. My wife and I have discussed it and we think that by the time she graduates from high school she will have grown out of this behavior," he said.

What if she kills herself in the meantime? What if she gets in the backseat of a car with three young men and you don't find her? Who is responsible for your daughter's behavior?" I asked again. "Are you, her parents, responsible for what she does? Are you willing to follow her around for the rest of her teenage years, attempting to correct her mistakes while feeling guilty for what she has done? That is a tremendous responsibility!"

"Well, perhaps it is just a phase that she is going through," said her mother. "Although recently we had some friends visit and we mixed some cocktails for them. When my husband's friend took a sip of his drink he kidded us because the drink was 'all water with no liquor.' My husband said that he had mixed it like he knew he liked it. His friend said that my husband should taste the drink. There was no liquor in the drink, for there was no liquor in the bottle. The liquor in the cabinet was all gone. Someone had emptied the bottles and filled them with colored water! We could not believe that someone would think that we were that stupid. But, we want you to know that we do not think it was our daughter. We just cannot believe that drugs are a problem in this case!" her mother said again.

"Our daughter has been making failing grades in school for the past several semesters. She has been skipping school and forging notes from us to her counselor. We are very concerned that she will have to repeat a grade and will not graduate from high school on schedule. We just cannot understand what has brought about this behavior change. She used to be so very different," her dad said softly.

"Have you had her to a physician recently? Perhaps there is something physically wrong with your daughter that is causing these problems?" I suggested.

"Yes, we took her to our family doctor and he said there was nothing wrong with her physically. He was the one that suggested that we bring her to the Outreach Program for treatment," said her dad.

"But Outreach is a drug abuse rehabilitation center for adolescents. Why would he suggest bringing her here if there is no drug problem?"

"I think she could have a problem like that," said her mom. "My husband does not agree with me. It just seems impossible that drugs could be the problem!"

"You know," her mom, continued, "I wanted to take my daughter to the mall last weekend to have lunch and shop for the day. My daughter said that she did not want to go with me. When I asked her why, she said that she did not want her friends to see her with me. That really hurt! I just do not know what could have done this to my daughter."

"Well, what do you suppose could have changed your daughter into this strange, angry, manipulative, hateful, resentful, foul-mouthed young person? Could it be that 'the devil made her do it'? Could it be that she has some 'mental problem'? Could it be a Communist plot to overthrow your family? What could be wrong? Is it not possible that chemicals have come into your child's life and have altered her behavior, her attitudes and her emotions? They can do that, you know. If it were a drug problem, then it would not be your fault. It could be a relief to find out that drugs are responsible for these changes in your daughter's behavior. We can treat chemical abuse. We can teach you how to help your child get un-abused by drugs and you can have your family back together once again. That is something worth considering."

Why couldn't the parents of this young girl understand what seemed very clear to me? Why were they choosing to close their eyes to what was going on? Would they have to suffer shame and guilt if they learned that their daughter had a mind of her own and that she can get into trouble with drugs even when her parents are doing the best they know how to do?

The father interrupted my thoughts. He said, "But we could not bring our daughter into treatment at this time because she would miss the end of her eighth year in school."

"But I thought you said she was skipping school and failing the eighth grade?" I questioned.

"Well, she is, but she might luck-out and pass anyway," her dad responded.

"Ah yes, I forgot for a moment that 'passing' is what we are interested in, not learning," I said.

"Anyway," her mother went on, "we have such a fun summer planned that we would not want any of the family to miss any of the vacation."

"Help me to understand why you are interested in entertaining the daughter that calls you filthy names and makes you drive your car in search of her in the middle of the night?"

"I guess that we just love her and want her to have a nice summer," her dad said. "It would be just awful if we brought her to Outreach for treatment and found she was not doing drugs. She might never speak to us again! I mean all that we know is that she has had a couple of beers in her life."

"She is fourteen years old! Were you drinking 'a couple of beers' and needing to be picked up from parties because you had too much too drink when you were fourteen? Were you calling your dad filthy names and did he want to knock your teeth out because of your language? Did you act like your daughter at age fourteen?"

"Well no!" said the dad, "but then, times are different now."

"So because times are different, you two have to be out of control with your daughter? You have to resort to wondering where she is at night? You have to wonder who is drinking your liquor without your permission? You have to wonder who breaks into your car to steal cigarettes? Is that how different it is today, or is it that alcohol and other drugs have changed your daughter's behavior to the point that you are all out of control?"

Her dad said, "You have really been kind to us. I think that we had better go home and think about what you have said, but I want to state again that we don't think that our daughter has a drug problem. I am just afraid that if we do something right now we might ruin her passing the eighth grade and ruin her summer vacation and she might never forgive us for that!"

"I don't blame you for being concerned parents. You and your daughter have a serious problem and you *all* need some professional help for sure. You came to a drug abuse rehabilitation center twice for advice and I really wonder why you did that. I believe that you suspect that your daughter has a drug problem but it seems too horrible to admit to yourself. You think that you could not withstand the shame that would go with the admission."

"Remember that you did not do drugs with your child. You did not buy drugs for your child. You did not recommend drug abuse to your child. You did not force your child to smoke cigarettes or drink alcohol. Perhaps her peers did that, but you did not. Her use or abuse is her fault and that is not your fault. You do not have the power to stop your daughter's insane behavior, and you could get the credit for saving her life! Your daughter would not like your taking charge, but she will appreciate your help when she is straight once again."

"Once my son got very angry at me for taking him to our family physician when he had an internal infection. He did not like shots and he saw no necessity to have one. I took him kicking and screaming because I knew that I was doing something that was in his best interest. You are facing the same thing. Your daughter is out of control from your point of view and from her own. Why else would she treat herself and you in this manner? Admit her to treatment because she needs it, not because she wants it!"

"It just seems like the wrong time to me, Dr. Brown! I want to give her more time to straighten herself out," her dad said.

"I understand that you are struggling with denial right now. I understand that when you faced your daughter for the first time in the nursery of the hospital where she was born you never once imagined her in a drug abuse center at age fourteen. I know that you would rather go on a happy family summer vacation than come into treatment at Outreach. Any sane parent would rather go on a happy summer vacation than go to drug counseling. I also know a family that would not face the fact that their child needed help and she is dead today from driving under the influence of drugs. I know another family that avoided treatment for their child and he shot himself to death while under the influence of drugs. Drugs allow humans to do things they would never do if drugs were not in their bodies. Please look at what is going on in your daughter's life and within your family. It looks to me like drugs are controlling lots of behaviors and you think that is too painful to admit."

"The moment you admit that drugs are a problem in your family is the moment that recovery will begin for all of you.

"Drugs have changed your family. You need to get drugs out of your family and restore it to sanity. I know you do not want to hear this, but I would be less than caring if I told you what you wanted to hear."

The parents thanked me for my time and left the office.

How do I reach people that are so very afraid of seeing what is right in front of them? How do I help parents to understand that children have minds of their own, they do what they want?

How did we get this way?

—DENIAL!

Food For Thought

- Our children have minds of their own. They may do what <u>they</u> want, not necessarily what <u>we</u> want. When they do what <u>they</u> want, what does that say about us, their parents?

- Are we capable of making sure our children follow in <u>our</u> footsteps? Can we insure they adopt our values, morals and preferences?

- Being best friends to our children is a popular role for many parents. "If I take exception to my sons' or daughters' plans and desires, they may never speak to me again. I cannot take that risk!" What role are you playing as a parent? How might you be more effective after reading this story? Please be specific.

The Night After Thanksgiving

So who's in charge?
 I am!
 What do you mean?
 What do you mean, what do you mean? I am in charge of *my* life and the way that I *think*!
 Tonight as my wife and I sat on our back patio, enjoying the cool Florida weather, the married couple in the rented house behind us was swearing at one another, screaming and breaking things in their house. She screamed, "F—k you, I'm leaving!" Then there was more pounding, more screaming and more swearing.
 They were each *controlling* the other and they were both *hurting* each other. Someone was *in charge* of the pain! Who was it?
 I blamed the male voice. I wanted to take charge, dial 9-1-1 and have someone stop the pain. I wanted to rescue the *helpless* female. I wanted to take the world in *my* hands and protect the victim in the situation.
 But, *who* is the *helpless* victim? Perhaps it is the one that *thinks* he or she is helpless.
 Is *she* helpless? Hell no! She just *thinks* she is helpless.
 She is as *powerful* as she wants to be. She does not have to suffer at the hands of a man who wants to control her. She screamed, "I'm leaving!" And then, she stayed, to fight, long into the night, and the next day.
 She *thinks* she deserves to be hurt? Her father hurt her mother and now a man is hurting her. That's how she makes sense of it all, that's how she continues to endure the suffering. "If it was good enough for my mother, it's good enough for me!"
 She refuses to think beyond what she has seen in her past. Her mother got beaten and now she gets beaten. What else is there for her?
 The fact is that *she* puts up with only that which *she* decides to put up with.
 I know better than to ever even think of hitting my wife! Marcia believes that she was *not* meant to be hurt and therefore she is *not* going to stand for such treatment.

So what's the difference?

The difference is in our *attitudes* and *beliefs*!

I've heard that since I was a little boy! People told me to *change my attitude!* They told me that *my attitude was the problem,* not what was happening to me. They said that my attitude was controlling my behavior, not the environment!

Tonight, I'd bet a dollar that the problem is *her husband.*

She thinks *she has to take it* and therefore she stays for more abuse.

She's got a *stinking* attitude for she does not have to stay. She does not have to be abused.

She has a *choice.* She has lots of choices.

Who is going to tell her? Who is she going to believe? Who can make her listen and understand? Why hasn't she listened before? What is wrong with her attitude that she cannot hear, or will not hear?

Why do I care? Why do I upset myself because she won't live like I want her to live?

I have made a living, for the past 30 years, suggesting to men, women, boys and girls, that *we all have choices* about how we are treated and what we must put up with in life. We have choices, lots of choices.

We do not have to endure *shitty situations* that we do not want to endure! Is that news to you?

We have choices about what we do and what we think!

We are *powerful* human beings and we can make powerful choices! We can get out of abusive situations! We can protect ourselves, care for ourselves, or offer ourselves to others to be abused.

It is uncomfortable to change! That is a neurological fact. Change brings conflict. That's a fact. But, have you ever thought that change can be *less* painful than staying where you are?

Oh the hell with it! You won't listen! You say that I *cannot understand because I am not in your situation.*

So stay where you are and suffer some more!

Just remember, one day when the pain gets really intense, that *you do not have to stay where you are and hurt! There are, whether you know it or not, other people in the world who will love you, care for you, and treat you with kindness, respect and gentleness, if you care enough about yourself to look for them. Give them a chance to find you.*

You take a risk staying where you are. Take a rational risk and get out!

Stop hating yourself!

Start loving yourself!

Change your *attitude* and change your behavior.
Someday soon you will thank yourself.
Change is possible. Happiness is possible. Love is possible. Love and happiness can come to you if you make yourself available.
Do it *differently* tonight, please.

Food For Thought

- "If I try harder I think I can get him to stop drinking! Perhaps there is something I am doing to make him like this. I can't give up now!" How are you in charge of how someone else behaves?

- Henry Ford said, "If you think you can't, you can't. If you think you can, you can!" Even The Little Engine That Could said, "I think I can, I think I can." And, he did! What is it that you think you can't? Do you suppose you really could?

- Do you suppose your ability to change can really come from thinking differently? Can simply the notion of, "I think I can," really make a significant difference?

Mister Ghost

Once upon a time, a three-year-old boy named Austin went to spend the weekend with his "Gam-maw." He liked to visit Gammaw because she gave him all her time and attention. Gammaw filled Austin's Sippy-Cup with grape juice; she gave him special treats from her cupboard to eat; she took him for rides in the wagon; and she read him stories from the many books she bought for him.

Austin liked his Gammaw, and he followed her through her house, watching her every move. Austin helped Gammaw pick up the fallen leaves from the potted tree on the back patio. He built roads out of blocks with Gammaw for his cars and trucks to run on. He shared cookies and milk in the kitchen with Gammaw several times each day. He loved to go for rides in the wagon, with Gammaw pulling him through the neighborhood.

The weather in Cape Coral, Florida, is always warm and sunny, so Austin is almost always able to talk Gammaw into a ride around the block. Austin is the happiest when Gammaw is leading him through the neighborhood where he can point out the many sights.

Austin is in love with boats and water. He was born in Florida, and early in his young life he learned that boats and water are fun. Two of his first words were "boat" and "water." Soon he was making a sentence with the words, "See the boat in the water!"

As Gammaw pulls Austin in the wagon, past houses in the neighborhood, Austin can spot neighbors' boats on trailers in their yards. His face lights up as he says, "See the boat! Boat in the water!" Whether the boat is in the water or not, Austin will say, "Boat in the water!"

In Cape Coral, there are lots of boats in neighborhood yards, so there is a great deal for a young sailor to get excited about. Austin never misses a chance to "See the boats!"

However, this was the weekend before Halloween. It meant that many yards were decorated with pumpkins, spiders, spider webs, more pumpkins, and ghosts. Austin was thrilled! He had boats to talk about, and he also had pumpkins, spiders, and ghosts to notice. He never missed a chance to show his Gammaw what was out there to see.

As Austin and Gammaw were getting close to Gammaw's home once again, Austin spotted a very large ghost hanging high in a tree. This was no ordinary ghost. It was very large and had a long flowing body blowing gently in the evening breeze. The ghost's face was easy to see. It had BIG eyes and a BIG, friendly smile that appeared to be looking right at Austin. Austin stopped the wagon to gaze at the friendly ghost. It was hard to take his eyes off this ghost for some reason. Austin was staring at the ghost, and the ghost was looking right back at Austin! It was as if they had met somewhere before...

Austin was impressed. He had seen the ghost...and the ghost had seen him.

Austin talked about the ghost the rest of the way home. When he got home he told Papa Dave about the ghost and how "Mister Ghost" was high up in a tree. He liked the ghost, and he thought the ghost liked him. He thought they were somehow friends.

That night Austin slept in a portable bed in the master bedroom with Gammaw and Papa Dave. He felt safer there than in a strange bedroom of his own. It was kind of different being away from home, in a strange bed, and Austin liked to sleep as close to his friend Gammaw as he could. She even put a special nightlight near his bed so he could see what was going on around him when everyone else was asleep. He liked it better that way!

This was going to be a special night for young Austin, but he didn't know it yet.

As Austin fell asleep, he started to dream...or was it really happening? Austin could not get his mind off Mister Ghost! He saw him up in the tree, alone and cold. He wanted to help him. He climbed out of his bed and found his way to Papa's garage. In the corner of the garage was a tall ladder. He would need to take the ladder with him to help his new friend. He put the ladder on Papa's antique wagon and headed quietly out of the garage. He did not want anyone to hear him leaving the house, or they would spoil his plan.

"Ooops," he said to himself as he left the garage, "I almost forgot! I need some scissors to cut Mister Ghost down from that tree." Back into Papa's garage he went, found some scissors on Papa's workbench, put them in the wagon along with the ladder, and headed for the next block once again.

It was dark, and there was only the light of the moon to help him navigate. It was a little scary, but Austin knew what he had to do. He had to find Mister Ghost and cut him down from the tree. He didn't want him to spend the night all alone and cold in the tree. He wanted to be Mister Ghost's friend!

After a couple of wrong turns, Austin spotted Mister Ghost! "There he is!" Austin exclaimed. "Now I can help Mister Ghost!"

Austin leaned Papa's ladder against the tree on the side where Mister Ghost was hanging. He started to climb up the ladder. He took his time climbing the ladder because it was a little scary being so far off the ground and all alone. He climbed one step at a time and hung on to the ladder with all his might. Soon Austin was face-to-face with Mister Ghost. He looked Mister Ghost in the eyes only to see a BIG smile appear on Mister Ghost's face. Austin knew that he was doing the right thing!

Austin said, "Mister Ghost, I am here to set you free! I brought Papa's scissors to cut you down." Mister Ghost appeared to smile even bigger when he heard Austin's words. Austin reached out with the scissors as far as he could and used all his strength to cut the string that was holding Mister Ghost to the branch of the tree above him. "There...I did it!" exclaimed Austin, as Mister Ghost gently floated to the ground.

Austin climbed back down the ladder to greet his new friend. Mister Ghost was already standing up next to the ladder and helped Austin with his last few steps to the ground. Mister Ghost wrapped his arms around Austin and gave him a big hug. He said, "Thanks a million, Austin, for getting me down from that tree! You are indeed my friend!"

Austin lit up with a great BIG smile, and so did Mister Ghost. The night seemed perfect somehow, and even the moon seemed brighter. All was great with Austin's world!

Austin explained that he had to get back to Gammaw's house before she or Papa woke up and found him missing. He said, "I have to hurry back to Gammaw's house right now!"

As Austin said these words, Mister Ghost's smile turned to a frown. Austin could not believe his eyes. "What is the matter, Mister Ghost?" said Austin "Why do you look so sad all of a sudden?"

Mister Ghost explained that he was happy to be down from the tree, but he had no place to sleep. Austin smiled a BIG smile and said, "You can come to Gammaw's house and sleep with me!!!"

Mister Ghost was once again happy. He smiled a BIG smile. He helped Austin load the ladder on Papa's wagon and joined Austin in pulling the wagon back to Gammaw's house.

Once in the garage, they put the ladder, scissors, and wagon back where Austin had found them. Then they closed the garage door tightly, quietly entered Gammaw's house, and found the master bedroom where Gammaw and Papa were fast asleep. Austin and Mister Ghost crawled into Austin's little bed and were fast asleep in no time at all.

Austin dreamed about his rescue of Mister Ghost. It was a grand rescue, and Austin was very proud of what he had done. Now Mister Ghost was safe, and Austin had a new friend.

In the morning when Papa and Gammaw awoke, Gammaw invited Austin to the kitchen for some grape juice and pancakes; two of Austin's most favorite treats. Austin whispered to his new friend that he ought to join the party in the kitchen. Mister Ghost did not hesitate. He was hungry too.

Austin shared his breakfast with Mister Ghost. Gammaw was amazed at how much Austin ate for breakfast that morning! She did not know that she was cooking pancakes for <u>two</u> people because Gammaw could not see Mister Ghost. Only Austin could see and hear Mister Ghost. And Austin liked it that way.

Austin and his new friend spent a wonderful day together. Mister Ghost was sure to follow everywhere Austin went. Austin shared all his treats and all his good times with his new friend.

All of a sudden it was Halloween morning. Mister Ghost announced to Austin that he had to leave him for a while. He would not tell Austin why he had to leave or where he was going. All of a sudden Mister Ghost was gone! Austin was immediately sad. He thought he would never be without Mister Ghost.

The rest of the day was not as much fun for Austin as the days before when Mister Ghost was around. Something seemed to be missing. Austin liked life better when his friend was with him.

Just when Austin was thinking that Mister Ghost had left him forever, he saw Gammaw's front door open and in came his buddy, Mister Ghost. He had something under his arm. It was some sort of package. Mister Ghost asked Austin to help him open the package. "Here Austin, this is a present just for you!" Inside was a costume. It was an exact copy of Mister Ghost! It was made for Austin, and it fit him perfectly.

"Wow," said Austin, "this is wonderful! I never thought I would have a chance to go trick-or-treating, and I never thought I would look just like my new best friend! This is super-duper!!"

Well, Mister Ghost and Austin went trick-or-treating that night. They walked and walked and walked together. They smiled and skipped and really had fun. They got lots of candy and treats wherever they went. The grown-ups all told Austin that he looked great. It was one of those perfect nights for sure.

"Austin," said Mister Ghost, "I want you to know that I am your friend. I will be your friend forever and ever and twenty-two days! I will be with you at all times. All you have to do is look for me, and I will be here. Whenever you need someone to talk to, or someone to help you, I will be here. You can count on me!"

Austin changed that Halloween Day! He smiles more. He is more pleasant to be around. He is more peaceful and relaxed. He knows that he is never, ever alone. Austin has a friend for life. Yes, Mister Ghost and Austin are buddies. That is the way it should be.

Food For Thought

- Imagination is a wonderful and powerful human ability. How have you used your imagination to help yourself?

- Did you have an imaginary friend when you were young? Describe your experience, please.

- Do you have an adult imaginary friend? How has this friend helped you, or let you down?

"Mom" Nelson

It was Orientation Week at Otterbein College in central Ohio. The new freshman class had come to campus a week early to move into the dorms, learn the layout of the campus, be rushed by fraternity and sorority actives, meet their professors and register for classes. It was an exciting and anxious time for each and every new freshman.

The fraternity parties, new dorm friends and trips to a local college hangout were the most impressive. There was also the young freshman majorette in the cafeteria line that made quite an impression on me as I remember. She was 5'2" tall, had short blonde hair, with large, round, blue eyes, and she was very outgoing indeed. Somehow I managed to always be right behind her in line for each and every breakfast, lunch and dinner. She was not only pretty she seemed most interested in my attention. That only seemed to reinforce the idea that I wanted to be where ever she was during those ten days of orientation. Not to mention the fact that the upperclassmen had warned me that as soon as the rest of the college students reported to campus, the freshman would no longer have any chance with the pretty coeds. The competition would be too much for us to stand.

Those days seemed far away at the moment.

There was a meeting in an hour in the Chapel with the Dean of Students. It was to be a State of the Union Address. The Dean was stern, although he did his best to welcome us to our new college life. He said that the admission's standards were a bit relaxed in that it was "easier to be admitted than it was to graduate." In fact he said that, "by Christmas, only one-third of those in attendance in Chapel that day would remain. The rest of the Freshman Class would be sent home because of poor academic performance." We had one semester to prove ourselves to those in power! I will never forget the Dean asking us to "look at the person on our right, and then look at the person on your left. Two of you will not be here after the Holidays!" That was not an exciting piece of news to ponder.

I had to wonder if I would be one of the fortunate people to still be on campus when the year ended?

One new friend, and impressive fraternity active, was a man named "Ruble." He sure seemed to know what was going on. He had lots of advice about almost every subject and he was willing to share it with any young freshman that would listen. He was clear about one issue. He said that Freshman English Composition was the course that was used to "weed out the Freshman Class!" And in particular, there was one professor who seemed to enjoy that process more than any other. Her name was Mrs. Margaret Nelson, not so affectionately known as "Mom." Ruble warned me to "stay away from her. And, at all cost, not to register for her English class!"

The last Saturday of Orientation Week was Registration Day. It took place in the campus gym. It was called a "scramble situation" in which the students came to the gym, en masse', and when the doors opened it was a free-for-all. Students went in all directions to line up in front of the professors they most wanted to take classes from, and then waited in line to see if they could get registered before the classes filled up and therefore closed.

I wanted to major in mathematics and minor in physics. I had heard of a couple of men who were especially talented in those areas and so I went straight to their lines. The lines were not as long as other's, for math was not as particularly popular a subject. Nevertheless, it took time to register for the courses that led to my major. And, worse than that, I <u>forgot</u> about the warnings from "Ruble" about "Mom" Nelson.

All of a sudden an immobilizing fear took over my body. I looked in the direction of the English Department lines and the Freshman English Composition Courses were all filled, with the exception of one. Mrs. Nelson was the only professor remaining with room for me!

Now that might not have been as bad as it appeared, but I did not have an impressive track record in English. For the best part of twelve years of public education, I had been told time and time again, that my handwriting was sloppy at best, that my spelling was not at all impressive, and that I could not write themes to acceptable academic levels. That past feedback, coupled now with thoughts of sitting in Mrs. Nelson's English class, made my feet feel very heavy indeed as I attempted to approach the desk where she was seated.

I really didn't want to be one of the two-thirds of the student body that would be leaving at the end of the first semester!

I finally approached Mrs. Nelson's desk and explained that, "I wanted to take her course." She was rather business-like as she signed my registration form and said, "I will see you Monday morning at 7:45, Mr. Brown."

Well Monday morning came and I walked into Mrs. Nelson's class before the required 7:45 a.m. bell. She was seated at her desk and seemed to watch each of us as we chose a place to spend the hour. When all the students were seated, Mrs.

Nelson closed the door and stood before us. She explained once again that this course was going to teach some of us how to become more proficient writers as well as weed out some of the less fortunate students. I was more nervous than ever before!

Then it happened! Mrs. Nelson explained that she wanted to get better acquainted with how well we could express ourselves on paper. "I want you to write a theme for me. Do the best job that you know how to do. I want you to write a theme about the most important character you have ever met. It is due on Friday!"

I clearly remember thinking that this might possibly be the last college theme I would ever be asked to write!

Friday came and my theme was complete. I chose to write about the coed that I met in the cafeteria line. I wrote about how exciting it was to meet a lovely creature such as she. She looked absolutely beautiful in the morning while waiting in line for breakfast. Her light blonde hair reflected the morning sun as though it was covered with diamond dust. And most importantly, I felt simply grand when she turned around, looked into my eyes, and said, "I was hoping you would find me here again this morning!" She was magical! I shared her, on paper, with Mrs. Nelson.

I handed in my theme. Mrs. Nelson explained that she had time to read the papers over the weekend and we could expect to get them returned to us on Monday morning.

Monday morning came. I appeared in class at 7:45 as expected. Mrs. Nelson handed back all the papers except one. I did not receive a theme! I raised my hand and said, "Mrs. Nelson, my name is David Brown, and I did not receive a theme from you?" Mrs. Nelson was quick to respond. She replied, "I want to see you personally after class!" Her face appeared stern and her voice seemed to lack any sign of warmth. I was very concerned, but also somehow relieved to realize that she was going to be critical of me privately.

I expected the worst!

After my peers had left the room, I approached Mrs. Nelson's Desk. She asked me be seated in the chair next to her desk. She took my paper out of a folder on her desk. She looked at the paper for a moment and then looked directly into my eyes. I will never forget the words she then spoke.

Mrs. Nelson said, "It had been many years since I have read such a theme! I wept when I read your thoughts regarding the young woman that you met during Orientation. You have a gift, David. You write beautifully. You gave me reason to believe that I was right there with you and your new friend. I was able to feel what you were feeling through your description. I asked another English professor to read your theme, and he agreed with me. You have a talent for writing."

I could hardly believe my ears. It was I, David Brown. I had impressed Mrs. Nelson with my writing. I could indeed write!

Since that very moment I have enjoyed writing.

Mrs. Nelson and I became grand friends. I worked hard to impress her even more with my work and she knew how to draw the effort out of me. She was the gifted person in the story indeed.

I wondered after graduation from college, if Mrs. Nelson somehow knew that I needed to hear something positive about myself, and talked to me as she did to motivate me, or did she really mean what she said. I suppose it didn't really matter. She had indeed made a very significant impression on me.

Thank you kindly, Mrs. Nelson!

Food For Thought

- Positive encouragement can be a powerful force in our lives. Was there a "Mom Nelson" in your life?

- What impact did her encouragement have on your life?

- Did you ever have the chance to thank your "Mom Nelson?" Perhaps it's not too late.

Kim

Southeastern Arizona was a new and wonderful place in which to live. I moved there from Cleveland, Ohio after the completion of a Master's Degree in Counseling. It was hard to believe that there was a place to live where the sun shown almost 360 days a year. The weather was warm and sunny, and the air was clean and fresh. It was simply glorious!

I moved to Arizona to help develop a new college in the desert. The college was located in the desert between two towns, one town was eight miles away and the other was twelve miles from the campus. The college was eight miles from the Mexican border. Forty miles east of the campus lay the Chiricahua Mountains, the former home of Cochise and Geronimo and the Chiricahua Apaches.

The Chiricahua Mountains rose 11,000 feet and were a great attraction to me. When it was 80 degrees at the college we could drive to the mountains and sled ride in the snow at 8,500 feet. Cleveland did not have scenery like this part of the country and the diverse terrain seemed amazing to me.

The mountains were also home to a rather interesting man. He was the "world's leading authority on spiders" and he was employed by the Museum of Natural History. He and his wife lived at, and operated, the research station in the Chiricahua Mountains. I was fascinated to meet Vince because I could not imagine what "the world's leading authority on spiders" might look like.

You see, in Cleveland we had only one kind of spider that I recall. They were called "Daddy Long-Legs," and were about as harmless a creature as one might find. One could not harm me if it chewed on me for an hour. But somehow, I grew up in Cleveland having learned to fear spiders. I didn't like them and did not want to share the same space with them!

I wondered what Vince would be like? Would he be covered with long, black and silver hair like the Arizona tarantula, and might he sleep up in the rafters of the research station, rather than in a comfortable bed? I got my chance to meet Vince and his wife the very first Thanksgiving recess from college. Another staff member and I took 60 students on a retreat from the college to the research station. It was a grand way to experience the mountains as well as meet the spider expert.

Both Vince and his wife were fun people to meet. They were very familiar with the out-of-doors, as well as being very hospitable hosts. They taught us a great deal about our temporary home. They also shared their travels with us as they had traveled all over the world searching for, and collecting, spiders to bring back to Arizona for their museum collection.

The research station contained literally thousands and thousands of both live and preserved spiders from around the world. They certainly came in all colors, shapes and sizes. It very much interested me to learn that Vince was spending his life collecting spiders. He seemed so normal. He was a pleasure to meet and study with.

We learned that Vince and his wife had plans to adopt a Korean girl. In fact, Vince was to fly to Los Angeles the day before Thanksgiving to meet his new daughter for the first time. He was going to bring her back to Arizona and both he and Kim would arrive at the research station on Thanksgiving Day. This added to the excitement of the holiday for all of us!

There was quite a bit of discussion about Kim and her arrival. Vince and his wife spoke no Korean, and Kim was reported to speak no English. That presented a problem from the very beginning. Vince and his wife, living in a fur trader's cabin at the research station, decided that they would do what the early Indians and white men used to do. They would give Kim a gift, the universal symbol for friendship. We all talked about what they ought to give their new five-year-old daughter upon her arrival in the mountains. Many items were suggested.

The day before Thanksgiving arrived and Vince left for California. The activities of the retreat continued. The weather at 8,000 feet was cold. The snow had accumulated to more than a foot. The mountains were a wonderfully beautiful place to spend the Thanksgiving Holiday after leaving the warmth of the desert below.

We all started to help prepare for the Thanksgiving dinner. There was a lot of work to be done with almost one hundred people expected for dinner. It was a personal thrill for me to be in Arizona, in the mountains, with sixty college students, and the staff from the research station. What a celebration we were having. And soon, there would be a new member of the family arriving from the other side of the world.

The students and staff worked very well together and soon it was time to eat the results of our collective efforts. Thanksgiving dinner was on the tables and people were starting to pass around the large bowls of food. Just as the eating started, the main doors to the dining room opened, and in walked Vince and Kim.

Everyone in the room looked in their direction, rose to their feet and applauded. Kim somehow seemed to know that she was the guest of honor for she grinned as wide as any little girl has ever grinned. It was indeed an exciting moment for all of us.

Vince and Kim joined us at the feast, and we all ate far past the point of sensibility. It was the best Thanksgiving dinner ever!

As the pie and coffee were being served, it was suggested that Vince give Kim her "welcome to the family" present. Vince was eager to comply. He left the room for a moment, and when he returned, he was carrying a small present with a very large bow. The box was about one foot square. He placed the package in front of Kim and motioned to her that the present was for her.

It appeared that Kim did not need to be told. She knew what a present was and she began to remove the brightly colored paper. Inside the paper was a terrarium. It was a glass box containing one of Vince's favorite possessions…a ten-year-old, female, Arizona, tarantula spider!

Students began to leave the dining room in all directions! No one asked anyone's permission, they just left!

I was shocked! I could not believe my eyes. "Why would this rational, kind, gentle man give this beautiful young child such a dangerous creature?" I could hardly believe my eyes! Vince removed the top of the glass box and took Kim's hand. He guided her right hand, palm up, into the top of the box. The spider began to climb onto her hand and up her wrist.

Kim beamed! She smiled a big smile. She looked pleased. Vince seemed to be very happy that his new daughter appeared happy with her gift. I continued to be very uncomfortable with what I was watching!

I could no longer contain myself! I asked Vince how it was possible for him to give Kim such a dangerous pet? He looked at me and smiled. He asked if I was serious. I said I was indeed serious. How could he do such a thing to his new daughter?

Vince explained that Kim's new pet was as dangerous as the creatures that flew through the air in Ohio, where I was born. He was talking about the ones that landed on human's bodies and sucked out their blood while injecting a toxin into their skin. They caused itching and welts and were a constant irritation in the summer. He was referring to mosquitoes. Vince explained that the spider was not a killer and that it was not dangerous to Kim. He said that one day Kim would squeeze the spider too hard or irritate it somehow and the spider would indeed bite her. She would get a small welt that would itch, and Kim would learn how to treat the spider so as not to be bitten again.

Vince picked up the spider and handed it to me. He asked me to hold it. I could not! I was afraid. I learned as a youngster that spiders were bad and not to be handled. Even though Vince said the spider could not hurt me I could not touch it.

I thought about it through the night. I believed Vince when he said the spider could not hurt me. I had learned to trust his word. I outweighed the spider by 180 pounds. It was really no threat to me, but my fear kept me away from it. It held all the power for the moment.

I decided to not let the spider win this contest. There was no rational reason to fear something that could not hurt me. I went to the research station lab the next morning and found Kim's spider. I put it on a lab table and placed my hand near the creature. It did not attack me! I placed my hand in the path of the spider and allowed it to walk over one of my fingers…then two fingers…and then my whole hand. I survived the experience!

The more I allowed the spider to touch me the more my fear seemed to subside. By talking to myself about the reality of the spider, while touching and surviving the experience, the less fearful I became. Therein was the lesson. By attacking my fear, by doing exactly what it was I was most afraid to do, and talking to myself about the reality of the situation, that being that the spider was not going to harm me, the fear was subsiding.

Perhaps Kim thought about the spider as an American child might think of a gerbil. They are cute, playful, fuzzy, entertaining, loveable, and friendly. If I had grown up to think of spiders in the same manner, then I would have understood Vince's gift to his new daughter and certainly would not have been afraid.

Dr. Carl Rogers, the world-renowned psychologist, said years ago, that it is not reality that controls how human beings behave, but rather <u>perceived</u> reality. Reality is not our guiding light. It is our <u>view</u> of reality that shapes our behavior.

His theory certainly held true in this case.

<u>Food For Thought</u>

- Do spiders have the ability to scare humans, or do some humans scare themselves about spiders? What's the difference? Why make a distinction about who scares whom?

- Did you ever have a fear that you overcame? How, specifically, did you do it?

- What advice can you share with someone else about overcoming fear?

"If You Do, What You've Always Done, You'll Get What You Always Got"

It was the day before Easter, and once again this year my wife was in the kitchen preparing an Easter ham for family and friends who were to have dinner with us on Easter. The house was filled with the aroma of good things cooking.

And like always, I wandered through the kitchen to see what "help" I could be in the process. I stood for a moment watching my wife cut the ends off the ham that was being prepared to meet the heat of the oven. She carefully cut through the ham bone and carefully cut a slice, several inches think, off both ends of the ham. I was not surprised for I had seen this process before. For some reason, this time I was more than curious. I asked my wife why she cut the ends off the ham. I didn't want to be critical of the process, for the outcome was not to be criticized! I simply wondered what removing the ends of the ham did in helping the ham cook to its' delicious conclusion.

I explained that I was not being critical. I simply wanted to know the reason for removing the ends of the ham? She explained, "This is the way my mother taught me to do it. I have always done it this way." I could attest to that fact myself. I could not argue with her logic.

The next day my mother-in-law came to dinner. When the conversation settled down a bit, I asked her if she cut the ends off her Easter ham when preparing it to be cooked. She said, "I have always done that, yes indeed." I asked if there was a particular reason why she did that. She said that there was a very good reason indeed. "My mother taught me to do it that way!"

It seemed that she did not know of a special culinary reason for the operation, other than her mother's habit of doing it.

So now my curiosity was piqued! I had to search out my mother-in-law's mother and ask her. This was accomplished some weeks later when we went to visit with her for an afternoon. I asked her to explain her personal recipe for preparing an Easter ham.

She told a very interesting story. She said that Grandpa, her husband, was a very paranoid man when it came to butchers and butcher shops. He would not allow Grandma to go to the butcher shop alone, because, "Butchers have a tendency to cheat woman and sell them less expensive cuts of meat than what they ask for. They are clever at it and it takes another man to beat them at their own game! So, I would tell Grandpa what I wanted from the butcher shop and he would always shop for me. But, Grandpa would always try to 'treat me' by buying cuts of meat that were larger than what I had asked for. This seemed to be his way of telling me that he loved me. When he shopped for me at Christmas, he would buy me a 25-pound turkey rather than the 15 to 20-pound turkey I requested. And, on Easter, he would buy me the largest ham he could find in the butcher shop. The hams were so large that they would not fit in my baking pan and I would always have to cut the ends off to get them to fit."

It seems that the practice of removing the ends of the ham carried on for three generations regardless of the size of the hams or the size of the pans.

__Food For Thought__

- "Old habits die hard," someone said, but they <u>can</u> indeed die. They can be modified by a change in our thinking. What habits have <u>you</u> changed? How did you do it? What did you think differently?

- Is there something you or your family has done for generations that "the story of the ham" brings to mind? Would you share your story, please?

Tootsie Pop Therapy

It was another warm, sunny morning in Southwest Florida, the kind we moved to Florida to enjoy. It was a pleasure just to be alive and headed to a new job.

I was hired to develop a Geriatric-Psychiatry Center for a local hospital, and this was the first day patients were to appear for treatment. The reason for the creation of the Center was that local citizens were in need of assistance. They were elderly, between the ages of 70 and 90, without family members in the area, or had no family members at all for support. They did not cook for themselves and were not getting their minimal daily nutritional requirements for good health. They needed medical care and it was impossible, or inconvenient for them to get to doctors' offices. They were sad or depressed and not seeking help. They lacked companionship and the friendship that they were once accustomed to as younger members of the community.

Neighbors, professionals in the community, and family members, referred the men and women to us. Once we had a group of forty grandmas and grandpas in need of help, we invited them to accept our transportation to the hospital on the first Monday morning of the month. They were going to be evaluated by a team of professionals, including our psychiatrist, social worker, geriatric nurse, and me, a psychologist. Together, our goal was to help each individual experience a happier, healthier existence.

The staff at the Center was excited! It had taken a lot of planning and work to arrive at Opening Day. Looking back, I assumed that we would be met with some eagerness on the part of the patients. We were ready, willing, and able to help. We valued personal health and happiness, and we wanted to share what we knew with those who would listen. Opening Day was an exciting event for the staff!

The bus that the hospital supplied to meet our transportation needs appeared at the entrance to the Center. Almost all the seats were occupied. Our staff met the bus and greeted the new arrivals with smiles and enthusiasm.

The women and men exiting the bus appeared to be less enthusiastic than we were at that moment. However, it was my job to greet them in our new Group Room and to explain our expectations and intentions. I imagined that they were somewhat apprehensive, as anyone might be when trying something new. I was a little apprehensive myself. But, I also imagined, with my skills, I would soon be able to put them at ease and we would get along well.

There were forty men and women in the group. The youngest member was 74 and the eldest was 89. I explained our new program and enthusiastically invited the group members to take an active role in counseling sessions, evaluations, and meals that were being offered. However, it soon became apparent that the members of this group would prefer to have been left alone, and not to have been bothered with traveling to the Center on this Monday morning! I remember feeling somewhat helpless. I asked the group some questions about their lives and activities, and almost none wanted to answer my questions. One man said that he would rather be home, sitting in his chair, staring out the window, waiting to die!

Day One was very difficult indeed! I used my best techniques to get the individuals in the group to talk with me. I offered them my skills and experience in changing their lives and attitudes, just a bit, to make life more enjoyable. I told them that I thought life did not have to hurt, and that I wanted to be a change agent in their lives. No matter what I said, for the most part they seemed not to want to cooperate with me.

Soon the first day was over and the bus took folks back to their homes. The staff spent several hours discussing the day and what we could do differently to get their attention. I remembered thinking of my Human Behavior classes with Dr. Viktor Frankl. I knew I had to tap into something memorable and positive, if even for a moment.

I remembered Kojak who used to enjoy a Tootsie Pop during times of stress while fulfilling his detective duties. Watching his television show reminded me how good a Tootsie Pop tasted as a youngster. I bought many a bag and took them to my office. I kept them in a jar on my desk and shared them with patients during therapy in my offices in Indiana, and Florida. They were a simple treat for us, and brought back many memories of pleasant times that had gone before. I was seldom, if ever, without those delicious candy suckers in my desk drawer or home pantry.

I was reminded of the power of a Tootsie Pop as I sat at home that day. I drove to my favorite store in the neighborhood and purchased a large, yellow box containing 100 Tootsie Pops. The next morning, after the forty members of my group had been seated in the Group Room, I entered the room to take my seat amongst them. Under my left arm was the yellow box of suckers. I sat down, placed the box on the seat next to me, and began to talk to the group.

I barely got one sentence out of my mouth, when a woman interrupted me, "Are those Tootsie Pops in that box?" I told her they were Tootsie Pops and that I like to keep them in my desk to be enjoyed during the day.

She asked, "Are you going to share them with us?" I said that was not my intention, actually.

She responded, "I have not had a Tootsie Pop since I was a little girl, and I would really like you to share one with me!"

One of the men interrupted her by saying, "I would like one also, but I would like to pick my own flavor!"

Almost without hesitation, various men and women sitting around me made it clear that they each wanted one! The mood of the group was indeed changing, and becoming much more positive.

I agreed to share the Tootsie Pops with the group. But, I wanted something in return. I explained that during the 5 or 10 minutes, while enjoying a Tootsie Pop, I wanted the individual group members to focus on the sweet taste of the sucker and think about memories of when they last enjoyed a Tootsie Pop. They agreed! The yellow box of Tootsie Pops was passed around the circle. Some men and women asked to be able to take two, one for when they were at home that night. I agreed. All forty participants took a sucker. One woman had a serious problem with diabetes and could not eat candy, but she asked to be able to take one anyway, just to have in her purse.

Soon we were all enjoying a Tootsie Pop together. The <u>sounds</u> of enjoying Tootsie Pops were coming from around the room. Smiles were appearing on faces, as the sweet candy brought back positive childhood memories of their last Tootsie Pops. Stories began to be told of instances when we went to the local candy shop, or grocery store, and adults in the family bought us a Tootsie Pop treat. I remembered going to the corner store for the construction workers building homes in our neighborhood. They sent me to the store for cold drinks, and in return, I could keep the soda bottles for the deposit. Most often I used the deposit money to purchase Tootsie Pops, a just reward indeed!

I must say that our Tootsie Pop experience was the turning point for most of the Grandmas and Grandpas in the group. We realized, together, that there <u>are</u> some enjoyable things to be experienced. There were Tootsie Pops, and more!

Once again, Tootsie Pops played a significant role in my professional life, as well as in the lives of the patients with whom I shared them. They have been, and continue to be, a memorable event in the lives of Americans, both young and not so young.

Food For Thought

- Remember those little, multi-colored dots of candy on long, white strips of paper? We ate the dots right off the paper. Do you remember the black, wax mustaches, and the red wax lips that could be worn and then chewed? Remember "Bull's Eyes?" Remember when there were a couple of multi-colored gumballs in the gumball machine, and if you got one of those, you could trade it in for a whole candy bar? How do you feel when you remember?

- The Tootsie Pop has "awesome power," or does it? Is there "power" in the candy sucker, or in the <u>minds</u> of those who remember a positive event in their lives? Most grandmas and grandpas remembered positive events wherein Tootsie Pops were included. One grandma, however, began to cry as she placed the Tootsie Pop in her mouth. She wept as mournfully as anyone I had ever seen! I put my arm around her and inquired as to what she was experiencing. She said, "I am crying because every time my father sexually abused me, he gave me a Tootsie Pop! This sucker brings back so many unhappy memories."

Yes I Can!

When I was a small boy I learned something very powerful. I learned I could make my mother happy or sad, my father happy or angry, my teacher smile or frown, and my sisters pleased or upset. When I behaved as I was expected, it was reported, "David was a good boy today." When I behaved in the opposite manner, I was told that I was a bad boy. It was clear I had control over how people around me felt emotionally and my behavior equaled my worth and value as a human being.

I spent most of the next thirty years attempting to take good emotional care of myself while protecting the people around me from feeling badly. I learned that I was in charge of how other people felt, and for the most part, they were in charge of how I felt.

From the time I was quite young, I had friends with whom I associated on a daily basis. Some days they liked me, and some days they did not. Some days I hurt their feelings, and some days they hurt mine. It was difficult, to say the least. When I thought I had done my very best, I was told I had hurt other people's feelings, and they were sore at me. I would apologize to a friend and he might say, "I cannot get over my hurt right away! It will take some time to get over this before we can be friends again." Friendships and other relationships were, and continued to be, difficult at best. It is difficult to take care of the way another person "feels" about me.

I remember the time I met a very pretty coed during my college freshman orientation. She was a woman that I wanted to get to know better. I stopped in a candy shop in town one day and bought her a box of assorted chocolates. I had them gift-wrapped. I took the present to the women's dorm and asked my potential friend to consider going to the movies with me. I handed her the box of candy and told her I bought a present for her. She acted very pleased with my gift. She said I was sweet to have done such a nice thing for her! I knew she was happy and it was clear to me, from previous learning, that I had indeed impressed this young woman. I had made her happy!

We actually dated for a couple of months and our relationship seemed to be improving as time went on. I was pleased and she seemed to enjoy having me around. One day I remembered how well the box of chocolates had worked several months before, so I returned to the same store to purchase an identical present. I returned to my friend's dorm that night; the same young man with the same box of candy. My expectation was to be met with welcome arms. What I didn't know was that she and her roommate had just recently decided to diet to "look better for their boyfriends." This time when she saw the candy, she became instantly upset. She said I was a very inconsiderate person to give a woman candy when she was dieting! She was angry and didn't want to see me for several days.

That was a confusing and frustrating time! The first time, the candy made her happy. This time it made her upset and angry. She blamed me for her feelings on both occasions. I was most certainly responsible for how she felt. Even her roommate told me that giving her candy was an inconsiderate thing to do!

That incident was just one of the many times in my life when it was very clear I was responsible for the feelings of other people. Some people went so far as to warn me they "wore their feelings on their sleeves," and I "must be careful not to hurt them."

What a mess indeed! I really wasn't sure how to feel the way I wanted and other people were warning me to tiptoe around in their space so as not to upset them. It was difficult enough to take care of myself without being emotionally responsible for those around me. It appeared that I was frequently hurting someone else's feelings, or so they reported. I spent lots of time and energy being concerned and careful not to say or do things that might cause other people to blame me for their hurt feelings.

Some days I felt really good about myself for I managed to please other people. Some days the opposite was the case. My value as a human being seemed to fluctuate like the Dow Jones Average. But so be it, that's the way it was.

Several years later in college, I began to study philosophy. I was fascinated with many of the books I was reading and professors with whom I studied. One day in class, Dr. George Axtelle, the founder of the John Dewey Society, presented an interesting idea. He said that he imagined most students had been raised on the premise that, "We were bad kids if we acted badly; and we were good kids if we behaved as expected." I could easily identify with that. He went on to say that he imagined that some days we were "good" and some days we were "bad,"…and some days we were "bad" in the morning and "good" by the time dad was to arrive home from work. I could also identify with that notion!

He said he had a better idea, one that would be difficult to understand and even more difficult to put into practice. He drew two circles on the board. The circle did not intersect nor did they touch one another. He made sure we saw them as completely separate. He even drew an imaginary wall between the two circles so we would know they were not related. He then explained the circle on the left is me, and the circle on the right is my behavior. He suggested that we see those two things as separate and different from one another. He said that I am not my behavior, and my behavior is not I.

Dr. Axtelle suggested that I am a valuable, fallible, human being. He said that I am a "human being" by definition, "fallible" because I am an imperfect organism that cannot avoid making mistakes, and "valuable" because I am alive and have potential to do good things for the society and me. He said that I am a V.F.H.B. from birth to death, and that I cannot change. "No matter what you do, David, you will always be a valuable, fallible, human being until the day you die." He suggested that we accept this definition and move on with more important aspects of our lives.

His message became clearer as he continued to lecture to us. He was telling us to stop rating ourselves. He said the only outcome of rating ourselves was to feel badly, and healthy people do not want to make themselves feel worse than absolutely necessary.

He then moved to the second circle, which he explained contained "my behavior." He said it made sense to rate behavior. Sometimes we do something well and we are proud of our accomplishments. Sometimes we make a mistake and it is well to note the mistake and take corrective action. We are all fallible human beings who must err and who make lots of mistakes. It is well to note the mistakes we make and evaluate them to see if there is a better and more efficient way to behave in the future. The message was to stop rating ourselves and only rate our behaviors. It made sense, he said, to dislike some of the things we do, but it makes no sense whatsoever to dislike ourselves.

It made sense to me! As a young child in school, when I was not in my seat when the bell rang, I would be punished. I ought to be taught to respect the wishes of the teacher and be in my seat when the bell rings if that is her rule, but there is no reason to consider me a rotten kid if I am not in my seat when the bell rings. I was not a rotten kid. I was a young boy who needed to be taught to follow classroom rules. Perhaps my behavior deserves evaluation and criticism, but I do not deserve to be insulted as a whole.

Listen to the difference. First, "David, you are a rotten kid for not being in your seat when the bell rings! Can't you do what you're told and follow the rules! What's the matter with you?" Or, "David, being in your seat is important to the smooth operation of this class. I would appreciate it if you would cooperate with me and make every effort to be in your seat when the bell rings. I respect you as a member of this class, and I am asking for your cooperation."

Dr. Axtelle said that we may behave poorly or badly, but we are not poor or bad people for having some so.

In that regard, I am reminded of a woman who came to me for counseling some years later. She said, "I am unworthy of happiness in my life because I am an illegitimate person." Her mother and father were not married at the time she was conceived. She had been told several times in her life that she was illegitimate. She looked like a full-fledged human being to me. She walked and talked like a human being. She was alive and responsive as I, but _she_ thought she was illegitimate. Therefore she treated herself like she was an unacceptable thing. This was even one step worse than my professor suggested. She was "bad" because her mother and father behaved "badly." She didn't even have the opportunity to earn her own badness!

I suggested that her parents' behavior did _not_ make her anything other than a V.F.H.B. I also suggested that if indeed she were "illegitimate," she would not exist, and there would be nothing further to discuss. She laughed when that idea was presented to her. Her belief did not change overnight, but with help and practice she was able to accept the new notion that she _is_ a legitimate, worthwhile human being who has the right and responsibility to help herself to happiness!

Food For Thought

- For whose feelings are _you_ responsible?

- Who blames _you_ for hurting _their_ feelings? How do they say you do it?

- What do you think differently now that you have read this story?

- Are you considering rating _only_ your _behavior_, and _not_ your _value_ as a human being? Would that be a significant change for you?

- You are an V.F.H.B!

Feelings

Feelings are talked about, sung about, written about, and are learned by each of us from birth to death. They are the joy we search for and the suffering we experience. Yet most human beings behave and talk as though feelings control <u>them</u>, rather than they control the feelings. We talk of feelings as being out of control; of being overcome with feelings; being disabled with feelings; punished by them; backed into a corner by them; and used by them. And yet, the truth is we <u>learn</u> to have the emotions that we harbor. Emotions are learned behaviors. We learn how to be angry, how to look when angry, how to sound when angry, who to be angry with, and how long to stay angry. We learn how to hurt, we learn how to look hurt, and we learn what to hurt ourselves about and how long to stay hurt. We learn to punish ourselves. We learn to punish ourselves when others behave in a manner that is contrary to what we expect. We believe that others should do what <u>we</u> want, rather than what <u>they</u> want. We punish ourselves because they have not done what we think they <u>should</u> have done.

Were I responsible for the creation of mankind, then perhaps, and only perhaps, would I be able to dictate to humans what they ought, should, must be doing at any particular time. However, if I am not the creator of mankind, then most likely each human being has the right to behave as he thinks he ought to behave. Therefore, I do <u>not</u> have the right to demand that my fellow man behave as <u>I</u> think he should. The next step in this thought process is, I also do not have to punish myself because my fellow man behaves as he thinks is rational for him.

There seems to be a "conflict" that humans are taught to experience. Conflict, as I define it, is the <u>difference</u> between what really is happening and what one would like to have happening. This is where our destructive emotions come into play. I see the world not as it really is, but colored by my attitudes and beliefs. As my beliefs become more subjective, based upon my opinions rather than reality, I suffer. As my beliefs become reality oriented and more in line with what is <u>really</u> happening, then I seem to suffer far less. The two circles move closer together. Those being the circle containing what I see as reality and the circle containing how I expect or want things in my life to be. The less subjectively I learn to think, and the more reality-oriented I become, the more my feelings reflect a true picture of what is really happening to me.

Take for example the common belief that one <u>must</u> be loved and approved of by everyone in order to be happy. If I believe this idea, then I have to suffer self-punishment when a fellow human being exercises his right not to like me or disapproves of me. I learn to think of myself as a less-valuable human being when an acquaintance chooses not to associate with me any longer. I choose to think less of myself when a loved one chooses to no longer love me. However, the reality of life is that I am not worth more or less, dependent on the number of friends, lovers, acquaintances, etc., that I have. I am still the fallible human being that I was when I was born and that I will continue to be. Should my family choose to no longer value being with me, I am still a valuable, worthwhile human being who can experience peace and happiness. My happiness is <u>not</u> dependent on who loves me and who approves of my behavior.

My happiness in life is dependent on the <u>thoughts</u> that I use to evaluate my perceptions of reality. The reality <u>is</u> that <u>I</u> control my feelings by what I think about me and about my relationships with others. If I choose to think and believe that <u>others</u> control how I feel, then I have to work on changing other people's behavior. If I rather choose to think and believe the reality that <u>I</u> make my own happiness by thinking and believing reality-oriented thoughts, then I find a new world filled with relative peace and happiness.

If I choose to think that it would be <u>nice</u> if people loved me and approved of my behavior, but don't <u>have</u> to love and approve of me, then I find I am freed of the "must" syndrome that is the cause of so much emotional pain. People may choose their own friends according to their own desires and wishes, and they do not have to choose me!

If I choose to think that people behave, as <u>they</u> want, and not as I want, then I can free myself from some negative feelings. Feelings can be an exciting part of the human experience, and they can also be the "hell" of life. The fact of the matter is that <u>we</u> control the amount of happiness or hell that we experience in life.

The human brain is the most important single organ in the human body. It is there we learn to respond to our environment and it is the brain that controls our behavior. However, my brain is only going to produce outcomes for me dependent on the information I choose to feed it. If I choose to believe lies and false information, then I experience feelings based on false data. My brain can believe that the world is flat if I choose to practice flat-world thoughts. My brain can believe that my mother and father <u>must</u> love and approve of me for me to be happy. But, just because I believe this idea does not make it true! If I believe it's true, then I will suffer when it does not happen. My brain may believe that should a loved one choose to live with someone else that my heart will break in two, but the belief does not make it true! I can believe that there is only one woman in the world that I can love, but my belief does not make it true!

I am the cause of my suffering, my negative emotions, and also my happiness and contentment. The more my thinking is in touch with REALITY, the less I will suffer. Because I LEARNED to have feelings that are self-destructive, I can RE-EDUCATE myself to have feelings that are more in my best interest.

The question as to whether I am dealing with what I THINK is real as opposed to what IS real is crucial to my mental health. The 18-year-old girl who once told me that "her mother could make her unhappy whenever she wanted to, and keep her that way as long as she wanted to" was expressing a very "real", but untrue belief. But as long as she chose to believe that idea, she had to feel badly when her mother disapproved of her behavior. When she learned that it was IMPOSSIBLE for her mother to make her angry, or to keep her that way, her life changed significantly. She learned that her belief was NOT in line with reality, but rather what she thought was reality. There is often a difference! She learned that she did not have to punish herself simply because her mother evaluated her behavior in a negative fashion. She did not need her mother's approval all of the time to be a happy, contented daughter. The daughter was responsible for her own emotional life, and her BELIEF SYSTEM about herself and her mother controlled it.

The woman who told me that "she could not go on without a husband" was expressing her opinion and NOT reality. The man who said "he had nothing to live for now that the only woman he could ever love had left him" was also expressing his own opinion and NOT reality.

Thinking objectively may be relatively new for some people, but it is not impossible. It may be a new mental (thinking) habit that can be learned with practice. It is up to each individual to PRACTICE the new thinking until the old belief is extinguished. The world is as it is, and we can choose to deal with it as it is and experience less misery, or we can choose to imagine the world differently from the way it is and suffer more.

If we look around us, it seems to be in vogue to suffer and express a significant degree of misery when life does not treat us as we prefer. But, just because other people expect us to be miserable when they are, is no reason for us to comply with their expectations!

Critics of this thesis object on the grounds that human beings become "machines that give up their emotional lives." This is an empty criticism. Human beings are EMOTIONAL beings who will continue to have emotions (feelings) as long as they are alive. Rather, what I believe is that because emotions are LEARNED behaviors, we can LEARN to have feelings that are more in our own best interest. WE can LEARN to be HAPPIER and less miserable. We can LEARN to give up the nonsense that we believe and replace our negative feelings with more pleasant feelings.

Can you remember a time when you did not have a lover and you were a worthwhile human being? Can you remember a time when a particular person did not love you and you were still worthwhile? If you can remember such times, then you can believe that the same is true now. If you cannot remember a time in the past when such was true, then you can learn for the first time that we are valuable and worthwhile with or without lovers, approvers, and certain particular friends.

We need to eat, drink water, keep relatively warm in the winter and cool in the summer, and what else? We can evaluate what it is that we REALLY NEED, versus what we only WANT. We do NOT have to have EVERYTHING we want in order to have peace and contentment! However, if we choose to believe that we NEED all those things that we only want, then we have to suffer more than necessary.

If you tell yourself that you want to be happier and less miserable, then also tell yourself that you CAN, whenever you choose to begin. Begin NOW. You CAN start to argue with yourself as to what you need versus what you only want. You can start by filtering or sifting your thoughts through an objective, factual, reality-oriented screen to allow yourself to have feelings that are more in line with reality. You can start by telling yourself that people have the right to behave, as they want. They do not have to behave, as you want. You don't have to believe all subjective opinions you now believe. You can start telling yourself that you have equal worth and value as much as any other human being around you. You can start feeling less miserable today by thinking your feelings are not controlled by other people. Your attitudes and beliefs make you feel the way you do! You can give-up your self-defeating attitudes and beliefs for ones that feel better, whenever you choose!!

You can start by thinking that life is filled with lots of choices. You can start feeling the way you want to feel anytime you choose to think objectively. The choice is yours to make. You can feel the way you want to feel anytime you want. You only have to be controlled by others as long as you choose to believe it is possible. Indeed, your feelings are really yours. You have created them and only you can keep them the way they are, or give them up for more comfortable feelings.

The CHOICE and the DECISION are YOURS…

HELP YOURSELF TO HAPPINESS…START TODAY.

Food For Thought

- Perception is a <u>combination</u> of what we sense <u>plus</u> our personal evaluation of our senses. It appears that we don't deal with reality; we deal with <u>perceived</u> reality. Our feelings are dependent on our perceived reality. Therefore our feelings are often exaggerated. When we reevaluate what has happened to us, our perceptions change, as do our feelings. When have you <u>reevaluated</u> an event in your life to understand it more accurately, and therefore have less unhappy feelings? Please be specific.

- "I am the cause of my suffering." Have you had this insight recently? What did you think or do differently?

- Our lives are indeed full of <u>choices</u>. What choices have you exercised recently to make positive changes in your life?

To Achieve My Dreams, Practice These ABC's

Accentuate the positive in my life. Develop a positive lifestyle.
Believe in my own personal potential for success.
Consider solving problems by seeking various points of view.
Do keep on making an effort to develop my talents and my potential.
Enjoy some moment in my life, each and everyday.
Family and friends are treasures just waiting to be discovered. Seek them out and cherish them.
Give more of myself than I planned to give.
Hold my dreams in high regard. Pursue them with enthusiasm.
Insure personal success by seeking support from those who will encourage me.
Just do something to move me closer to my goals, each and every day.
Keep on working!
Love myself too.
Make rational things happen for me.
Nice things happen to me when I am honest, trustworthy and dependable.
Open my eyes wide and see life's events as they really are. Be reality oriented.
Practice produces improvement and mastery.
Quietly search my thoughts for the positive, strong, calm and loving me.
Read, study and master those subjects that will help me realize my goals.
Start progress toward my goals…now!
Take control of my life today…this very moment.
Understand my goals, and me, and then make an effort to understand others.
Visualize my personal success. Visualize myself achieving my goals.
Work for success. No one ever drowned in his or her own sweat!
Xcelent efforts produce excellent results.
You and I are unique, worthwhile, loveable, special, powerful, and trainable.
Zero in on my target and help myself to success.

About The Author

David A. Brown, Ph.D., NCC, CCMHC.

Dr. David A. Brown has extensive educational preparation and professional experience in the fields of human behavior, counseling, innovations in education, program design and administration, and consultation and education. He has been a secondary school and university administrator; a college counselor and professor; the author, developer and director of grants for the United States Office of Education, the Office of Economic Opportunity, and E.S.E.A. Title III utilizing educational innovations; the director of comprehensive mental health centers; a counselor and consultant in Rational Emotive Behavioral Therapy; a school psychologist; and the director of operations for a Dislocated Workers Pilot Project with the Job Training Partnership Act. He has been the author and developer, as well as executive and clinical director, of an intensive, long-term, family-oriented, adolescent, drug rehabilitation treatment program in Florida. He has had more than 30 years of successes in encounters with drug abusers, would-be suicides, managers unable to cope, couples with marital problems, and juveniles with aberrant behavior problems.

Dr. Brown has developed and led successful experiential training programs in the Florida swamps to resolve interpersonal and intrapersonal relationship problems among high school students in high-risk areas for E.S.E.A. Title III. He has led groups of 300 pharmacists through personal conflict resolution experiences, as well as groups of neighborhood women and men in emotional survival encounters. Rational living, stress management, conflict resolution, and problem solving workshops were presented to industrial managers, school psychologists, college students, counselors and administrators, and J.T.P.A. participants with exciting success. Stress management, Rational Emotive Behavioral Therapy, and rational use of hypnosis are topics Dr. Brown has presented at numerous state and national conferences, service clubs, Chamber of Commerce, and other professional meetings.

Dr. Brown is author of the book, <u>The Pocket Therapist</u>, and has published numerous articles regarding the practical application of rational thinking.

Dr. Brown earned a Ph.D. in Leadership and Human Behavior from the United States International University in San Diego, California; an M.A. in Counseling from John Carroll University in Cleveland, Ohio; and a B.S. degree in Mathematics and Education from Otterbein College in Westerville, Ohio. He completed intensive postdoctoral work at the Rational Behavior Therapy Center of the University of Kentucky, College of Medicine in Lexington, Kentucky, and at the Outward Bound School in Morganton, North Carolina.

He is board certified by the National Academy of Certified Clinical Mental Health Counselors and the National Board for Certified Counselors, Inc. He is certified in Rational Emotive Behavior Therapy by the Rational Behavioral Therapy Center of the University of Kentucky, College of Medicine. He has served as Adjunct Instructor at Indiana University, Ball State University, Indiana Vocational-Technical College, and Edison Community College.

Dr. Brown is a Professor of Psychology at International College in Fort Myers, Florida. He particularly enjoys working with students in the areas of critical and rational thinking.

0-595-30542-3